Routledge Revivals

Russia and Peace

This book, first published in 1923, endeavoured to provide a brief account of the social and economic conditions in Russia at the beginning of the twentieth century. *Russia and Peace* discusses the interest in Russia shown by other countries, the country's economic development, and the social problems it was experiencing at the time. This book will be of interest to students of history.

Russia and Peace

Dr. Fridtjof Nansen

Routledge
Taylor & Francis Group

First published in 1923
by George Allen & Unwin

This edition first published in 2015 by Routledge
4 Park Square, Milton Park, Abingdon, Oxon OX14 4RN
and by Routledge
605 Third Avenue, New York, NY 10017

Routledge is an imprint of the Taylor & Francis Group, an informa business

Publisher's Note
The publisher has gone to great lengths to ensure the quality of this reprint but points out that some imperfections in the original copies may be apparent.

Disclaimer
The publisher has made every effort to trace copyright holders and welcomes correspondence from those they have been unable to contact.

A Library of Congress record exists under LC control number: 24002642

ISBN 13: 978-1-138-91073-7 (hbk)
ISBN 13: 978-1-315-69325-5 (ebk)

RUSSIA & PEACE

BY

DR. FRIDTJOF NANSEN

LONDON: GEORGE ALLEN & UNWIN LTD.
RUSKIN HOUSE, 40 MUSEUM STREET, W.C. 1

First published in 1923

Printed in Great Britain by
UNWIN BROTHERS, LIMITED, THE GRESHAM PRESS, LONDON AND WOKING

PREFACE

THE more one sees of the unbounded incompetence and national self-righteousness everywhere so blatantly manifest to-day, the more clearly does one become convinced that the first condition for finding a way—if a way there be—out of Europe's present confusion and advancing disintegration must be the attainment of a better mutual knowledge and understanding between its various peoples.

Another people's outlook, actions, and conditions generally, should be judged as far as possible by the norm of its own psychology, way of thinking, and preconceptions, and not by our own. This is surely the first and chief condition for being able to understand, and yet it is the one sinned against most often, indeed daily, and not least in the case of Russia and Russian affairs.

In this book the endeavour has been made to render, without prejudice, passion or partisanship, a brief account of the existing social, and especially economic, conditions in this vast and unhappy country, in the light of my impressions and those of my collaborators during the years that we have worked there, and of the information that we have obtained from the sources which seemed to be most reliable.

That these brief impressions make no claim to be exhaustive in any direction, goes without saying ; the immense Russian problem is far too involved and complex for that to be possible. Their aim is to help in laying the foundation for a more objective comprehension of present-day Russia and her future possibilities.

During the last decade the attitude towards Russia has changed in a very remarkable way. Before the Great War she figured as the huge menacing bugbear of the East, the barbaric despotism, the aggressive power, the great Slav peril to Western Europe and its civilisation. In particular, the treacherous oppression of the Finnish people gave Scandinavians a warning of what they could expect if they came under the iron Russian heel.

France's alliance with the " barbaric despotism " of the East was regarded as treason against the traditions of France, representing as she did the fight for liberty and the rights of man. Nowhere was this view more commonly prevalent than in Germany.

Then the World War broke out, and the Germans proclaimed that Germany's armies were really championing the cause of Europe, and the Scandinavian nations in particular, against the barbarism of the East.

But the points of view have veered round. No longer do we detect in Germany any widespread feeling that Russia is the great menace to be kept at bay ; if anything, the opposite view is held, and that, too, whether the Russian realm is contemplated as permanently Bolshevik, or as potentially Tsarist.

On the other hand, the nations farther to the west of Europe maintain a more hostile attitude towards Russia. In spite of the great services which the people of Russia rendered, at fearful cost to themselves, to the Western Powers during the most critical days of the war, the Governments of the West now seem disposed to let the Russian nation perish because it is subject to a Government to whose methods and terrorism they cannot reconcile themselves.

All this is essentially a matter of politics. But what is needed now is to try to get on, without paying heed to these changeable political moods, to an objective grasp of the facts as they really exist and must develop.

It is clear that Russia, conceived as a factor in the development of world civilisation, with its great intellectual and material importance in the world's domestic economy, cannot in the long run remain in bondage to shifting political systems, especially when these are largely imported from without.

A people's development strikes deeper roots ; a people is a living organism, with its own inner life, and in the long run it will refuse to be held in check or directed by fortuitous rulers, even though these should succeed in putting forward or retarding the clock of evolution for a time.

All Governments are transitory. The people and the soul of the people endure.

Doubts may be entertained regarding the future of Western Europe and West European civilisation ; but there can hardly be room for doubt that the Russian people has a great future before it, and a great mission to fulfil in the further life of Europe and the world.

Even as the expanse of Russian and Siberian plains holds immense potentialities in its great treasures of wholly virgin or only partially cultivated land, so does the Russian people contain great reserve forces of unused intellectual and moral power.

Russia's civilisation has not yet burst forth into blossom: it still belongs to the future.

The civilisation of Russia, as we have known it hitherto under the Romanoffs, has certainly not been Russian. It was a thin, West-European veneer, imported and renewed from without, just as its centre of culture, St. Petersburg, was merely an extremely uninspired copy of Europe, executed in stucco and plaster.

Only when one's eyes catch a first glimpse of Moscow, with the Kremlin's wonderful walls and towers, rising amid the surrounding plains, does one feel oneself on the threshold of another civilisation. This is no longer Europe, nor yet the Orient ; it is Russia.

Again, Bolshevism cannot be said to be really Russian. While its inner mechanism is more or less a copy of Tsardom turned upside down, the revolution itself was modelled, down to the smallest detail, on Europe, just as its theory, Marxism, was almost directly imported thence. But the idealism—the remarkable capacity for devotion by which it is largely sustained—is genuinely Russian.

Not yet has the soul of the Russian people been able to cast off the yoke of Western Europe and to achieve its free development ; not yet has it found a way to express *its own* truth. But its time will come.

When we read the literature of Russia, and perhaps even more when we listen to the national music of the Russian people, its strange charm, vibrant with the suppressed glow of passion, makes us conscious of the mighty, stirring echoes of melancholy from the limitless steppes, from the unknown depths of an alien existence ; we seem to hear a soul still in bondage utter its eternal yearning for liberty, and deep down in that soul we recognise a world still unborn.

One cannot be brought into close association with this great people, in prosperity or adversity, without feeling an affection for it and acquiring faith in its possibilities.

One must needs admire its stoical fortitude and boundless resignation, which may prove a weakness in time of development, but which is its great strength in the day of misfortune. Even against our will we are attracted by the high-strung emotionalism of its character, which may easily lead to excesses, but nevertheless bestows that remarkable gift of devotion and unhesitating readiness for sacrifice even unto death on behalf of its ideals or ideas, which we meet with again and again.

Only think of the Russian Nihilists. We were repelled by their methods of terrorism ; but we could not but admire their idealism and their utter self-sacrifice. The same spirit of exaggeration has found expression now in connection with Bolshevism, and it still arouses fear in us by its uncompromising terrorism.

It appears probable to me that not only will Russia some day, and at a date not far distant, save Europe in things material, but that the sorely needed spiritual renewal will also come from there.

And if that is so, there would seem to be every call for Western Europe, at this moment above all, to pay very close attention both to the Russian people and to the rapidly changing conditions in their vast country.

FRIDTJOF NANSEN.

CONTENTS

RUSSIA AND PEACE

CHAPTER I

RUSSIA AND THE ECONOMIC EQUILIBRIUM OF EUROPE

IN these days there is an uncanny, debilitating suspicion in the air that the old world is sick, that the civilisation and the social organisation of the West have gone into liquidation, and that its peoples' vitality has broken down.

It seemed reasonable to expect that when the four years' bloodstained nightmare of the World War was at length ended, the peoples of Europe would resolutely pull themselves together, and unite all their forces in the reconstructive labours of peace ; and it was hoped that following on the great effort of rebuilding all that had been smashed to ruins, and of paying the overwhelming debts incurred by the various nations, a new era of prosperity would dawn for the countries of the West.

But nothing of the kind has happened. The hurricane of war has by no means cleared the air.

We hoped for " a disarmament of men's minds," but the fell crop of hostility and national hatred is shooting up and spreading worse than ever between former enemies, and even former allies.

Disorder and insecurity are growing on all sides, and in several continents, while the feeling of solidarity appears daily to become weaker throughout our whole suffering human race.

Amid black storm clouds the Demon of War seems to hover again over stricken Europe, driving the unresisting nations onward to the abyss.

Everything that happens merely seems to hasten the catastrophe.

We looked forward to peaceable trade relations, we wanted to improve State finance, to stabilise the exchange ; but see what it has come to. Surely things were never as bad as now, and we look in vain for any serious attempt at international combination in order to solve the difficulties together. Repelled by the international chaos and insecurity, each people prefers to rely upon itself. This policy of distrust and isolation can only result in making the position radically worse.

If one had the impression that the Governments of Europe had done all that lay in their power to restore peace and to reconstitute the economic life of nations upon a sound foundation—then would one indeed lose all faith in the future.

Fortunately, that is very far from being the case. Fortunately, we can convince ourselves, by a rapid retrospect, that the fact has been that Europe has been suffering from an utterly absurd system of government, and we may be thankful that the damage done to it has not been still greater.

Who would dare declare that the years we have lately passed through have impressed him as being a period of rational thought, a time of intense and carefully planned work?

Europe emerged from the terrific affray mortally wounded and economically exhausted. Did we forthwith try to economise our strength in order to hasten a return to health? Did we do all we could to avoid the dangerous dissensions, to make the most of such strength as was left, and to develop and exploit such possibilities as still remained?

We have preferred to talk politics. Every problem has been rendered more difficult by deferring its solution, partly through laziness or lack of initiative, and partly through fear of incurring responsibility.

Innumerable conferences failed to secure an objective study of the various problems at the hands of Ministers and experts who were bent upon obtaining as quickly as possible decisions that would satisfy all parties. The negotiators were for the most part diplomatists and politicians who were outside international economic life, and who were much more taken up with their own, their party's or their country's position, than with measures to heal the deep-seated malady of Europe—men who, if anything, have made bad worse by their haphazard settlements, or have omitted to settle the most vital questions of all.

The political life of Europe, as it has developed since the armistice, presents a truly discouraging picture of uncertainty, indecision and incompetence; and above all of *bluff*. It is not at all surprising, indeed, that this regime has failed, at any rate as far as economics go, to secure anything whatever of value for Europe.

Only one thing could, only one thing still can save Europe: it is *work*, methodical, peaceable work. And in so much as the States of the Old Continent are dependent upon each other to a degree that the war threw into sharper relief, the reorganisation of Europe's work would mean the restoration of normal economic relations, permitting each country to organise its home activities in proper relation to the activities and possibilities of other countries. Europe cannot expect to thrive until it again becomes an economic organism instead of a mere aggregate of ill-assorted particles.

National policy tends to make each country into a unit which is as far as possible self-sufficient, by securing for it whatever it may need, through the medium of political expedients such as annexations, alliances, or the creation of spheres of interest.

In the period of international economics in which we live, the results of this policy are almost always negative, and have the sole effect of enfeebling the nation which imagines it can be self-sufficing.

The only policy which can save Europe is that which resolutely regards all problems from an international economic point of view, and which in every case seeks the solution which is most favourable for the resumption of work all round, which means the expansion of European production generally, and of the capacity to distribute what is produced.

At the present moment the nations of Europe are living in a state of grim economic anarchy. England is groaning beneath a fearful burden of unemployment, whereas France is suffering from a shortage of labour. The German rate of exchange rushes headlong down its giddy descent, to rise again all of a sudden as the result of a mere financial manœuvre initiated by the Reichsbank, after which it again rushes downwards. There is no sense in all this, and it ought to have been avoided, but it is obvious that normal conditions cannot be restored on the trade-market, any more than they can on the labour-market and the money-market, until the various countries are mutually connected again on the principle of communicating vessels.

Starting from this European point of view I shall endeavour to analyse the Russian problem.

European Russia has an area which is about half that of the whole of Europe. Her inhabitants, amounting to over a hundred million, form by far the most numerous continental people. Her fruitful lands were formerly to a great extent Europe's granaries, besides producing other necessaries. As a market, Russia possessed great importance for European industry.

No one who looks ahead a little, can suppose that we could cut off Russia from Europe and leave her to look after herself, without this exercising a decisive influence on the prosperity and future prospects of the whole European community.

A few figures will illustrate this. If we only take

the four most important cereals—wheat, rye, barley and oats—we find that before the war, in the years 1909-1913, the cultivated area—corn lands—in European Russia alone amounted to 81·7 million hectares (1 hectare = 2·6 acres), or more than a third (34 per cent.) of the total area of corn land in the whole world, which was about 240 million hectares.

European Russia's annual production (1909-1913) of the four cereals together was 65 million tons, or more than one-fourth (27 per cent.) of the entire world's annual corn production, which was about 242 million tons. If we add Asiatic Russia, Russia's aggregate annual production was 72 million tons. By way of comparison I may mention that the annual yield of corn in Canada, U.S.A. and the Argentine together came to about 67 million tons.

Russia's annual export of corn was 8·7 million tons, or more than the aggregate export of corn from Canada, U.S.A. and Argentine whence Europe now receives practically all its imports. The exports from these three countries amounted together to 7·7 million tons per annum.

It is sometimes said that Russia, prior to the war, exported more corn than it could really afford to do, as the peasants retained too small a quantity to satisfy reasonable requirements ; and therefore one ought not to expect nearly so large exports in the future as in the past.

On the other hand it should be noted that in spite of Russia's fertile soil, the average yield was only about 700 kilogrammes per hectare. A slight improvement in Russia's extremely primitive agriculture ought therefore to increase her production and exports to a very considerable extent.

What, then, are we to say of Russia to-day? Is she or can she become an essential factor in our economic life? Is she willing or competent to co-operate in restoring the economic equilibrium of Europe and in so doing to co-operate in restoring peace? These are the questions that we must try to answer, by passing in review the several aspects of Russian life.

In this chapter I shall confine myself for the present to emphasising the fact that Russia herself really seems to possess the conditions for adopting that economic and non-political view which has been already indicated as necessary. In the course of the Bolshevik revolution and during the long-continued blockade due to the war, she has amply experienced the impossibility of living without buying from other countries. She has also been fully convinced that in order to buy it is necessary to sell. Thus the restoration of uninterrupted and undisturbed economic relations of exchange with other countries became the leading aim of her policy.

Russia has purchased this experience at a dearer price than any other country in Europe, since she has had to pass through the almost complete destruction of her industry and her trade in order to acquire it. This very ruin of her economic life is what has brought about the reawakening which we now seem to discern, and has caused Russia to understand the necessity of abandoning political in favour of economic methods.

In the course of the conversations which I had in January and February of this year, in Moscow with a number of leading men in the Russian Government, I very strongly received the impression that the question which exercised them more than any other was the question of Russia's economic reconstruction and the restoration of normal economic relations with foreign countries.

M. Trotzky, Peoples Commissary for Defence, assured me of the Government's genuine desire to maintain peace and foster methodical work.

> Russia wants peace (he said), she has too much to do at home in restoring her own shattered finances to be able to think of war. For this difficult work she needs the labour of her whole population.
>
> Russia would nothing rather than to be able to cut down her army largely. She has proposed to reduce it to two hundred thousand men on condition that the other countries also effected a similar reduction. This proposal was not accepted.
>
> During these last weeks the events in the Ruhr have brought in a new factor, making possible an invasion of Russia by Poland and Roumania, as soon as they feel sure that they will not be attacked in the rear. In spite of this danger Russia has not delayed by one hour the carrying out of the demobilisation which she had decided on, by which the army was reduced from 800,000 to 600,000. The troops that we have under the colours to-day are less than half of the standing army in peace time under the regime of the Tsar. Is not that a sufficiently clear proof of Russia's desire for peace ?
>
> Part of Russia's programme is the formation of a force of militia, something like what Switzerland has ; but up to the present the situation has not allowed this programme

to be realised. Complete disarmament could not be contemplated before the day when Europe united in a federation of states, which offers the sole means of withstanding America's economic hegemony.

If general demobilisation can be carried out, Russia will propose an international disarmament commission.

The Red Army was a heavy burden for the country at the time when we had to fight on all fronts and when our effective forces amounted to several million men ("Five and a half millions in the time of our worst misery," Trotzky said).

To-day we only keep up the minimum number of troops which are unavoidably necessary to maintain our independence. On account of the heavy reduction of the army it is impossible for the soldiers to take part in the important work of economic reconstruction to the same extent as formerly when the army was larger. Nevertheless all commanders of troops have been given orders to help the peasants as far as they may be able with men and horses, in the places where they are stationed. In many cases regiments till their own fields themselves, and that is also a way of assisting in the work of general agricultural improvement.

Our great national effort aims at reconstructing the agriculture, industry, and trade of Russia, and we are convinced of the need of a peaceful economic renascence in all countries. Unfortunately Europe really seems to be animated by less peaceable tendencies.

I have quoted these observations by M. Trotzky because they show that even the military Soviet circles are aware of the fundamental importance of the economic factor. And this view will naturally prevail with far more cogent reason in the departments of the Russian Government which are responsible for the all-round reconstruction of the country.

CHAPTER II

THE FLUCTUATING INTEREST IN RUSSIA SHOWN BY FOREIGN COUNTRIES

It is important to note how up to the present other countries have failed to investigate the Russian problem from the point of view of general European economics.

When the Versailles Treaty was made, the Russian factor was entirely neglected. Not only so, but did not its authors overlook, or at any rate give the impression of overlooking, the nearly three hundred thousand Russian war-prisoners who were still to be found round about in Central and Western Europe?

I am compelled to add, however, that when the Supreme Council at that time decided to pursue the negative policy of the "sanitary cordon" and the "blockade" in regard to Russia, the explanation might be found quite as much in the attitude of the Soviet Government and in the attitude of the Russian emigrants and anti-Bolshevik sections as in the feelings that the other peoples of Europe cherished towards the Bolshevik administration. It will be remembered that the proposed meeting on the Island of

Prinkipo came to nothing on account of the disinclination for peace shown by the anti-Bolshevik Russians.

Knowing the scarcity which even then prevailed in Russia, especially its large towns, I conferred with Mr. Herbert Hoover in the spring of 1919 in Paris regarding what could be done to come to the assistance of the Russian people.

We agreed that a proposal ought to be submitted to the Supreme Council, for the formation of an organisation to supply Russia with food and other necessaries, against payment in the form of whatever export-goods of value were available. America was ready, through Mr. Hoover, to accord the necessary credit in the form of goods for starting the venture. The organisation would be responsible for seeing that the goods imported into Russia were distributed without political prejudice of any kind whatever.

On April 3, 1919, I sent the following letter to President Wilson, and similar letters to each of the three members of the Supreme Council:

MY DEAR MR. PRESIDENT,

The present food situation in Russia, where hundreds of thousands of people are dying monthly from sheer starvation and disease, is one of the problems now uppermost in all men's minds. As it appears that no solution of this food and disease question has so far been reached in any direction, I would like to make a suggestion from a neutral point of view for the alleviation of this gigantic misery, on purely humanitarian grounds.

It would appear to me possible to organise a purely humanitarian Commission for the provisioning of Russia, the food-stuffs and medical supplies to be paid for perhaps to some considerable extent by Russia itself, the justice of distribution to be guaranteed by such a Commission, the membership of the Commission to be comprised of Norwegian, Swedish, and possibly Dutch, Danish and Swiss nationalities. It does not appear that the existing authorities in Russia would refuse the intervention of such a Commission of wholly non-political order, devoted solely to the humanitarian purpose of saving life. If thus organised upon the lines of the Belgian Relief Commission, it would raise no question of political recognition or negotiations between the Allies and the existing authorities in Russia.

I recognise keenly the large political issues involved, and I would be glad to know under what conditions you would approve such an enterprise and whether such Commission could look for actual support in finance, shipping and food and medical supplies from your Government.

I have sent similar letters to M. Clemenceau, M. Lloyd George, and M. Orlando, in the hope that they will accord the matter the attention which so serious a situation deserves.

Believe me, etc.

FRIDTJOF NANSEN.

This proposal immediately received warm support in various quarters, but strong opposition in others. After it had been discussed very fully, not least by the French, I received on April 17, 1919, the following answer from the Supreme Council :

DEAR SIR,

The misery and suffering in Russia described in your letter of April 3rd appeals to the sympathies of all peoples. It is shocking to humanity that millions of men, women and children lack the food and the necessities which make life endurable.

The Governments and peoples whom we represent would be glad to co-operate, without thought of political, military or financial advantage, in any proposal which would relieve this situation in Russia. It seems to us that such a Commission as you propose would offer a practical means of achieving the beneficent results you have in view, and could not, either in its conception or its operation, be considered as having any other aim than the " humanitarian purpose of saving life."

There are great difficulties to be overcome, political difficulties, owing to the existing situation in Russia, and difficulties of supply and transport. But if the existing local Governments of Russia are as willing as the Governments and peoples whom we represent to see succour and relief given to the stricken peoples of Russia, no political obstacle will remain. There will remain, however, the difficulties of supply, finance and transport which we have mentioned, and also the problem of distribution in Russia itself. The problem of supply we can ourselves hope to solve, in connection with the advice and co-operation of such a Commission as you propose. The problem of finance would seem to us to fall upon the Russian authorities. The problem of transport of supplies to Russia we can hope to meet with the assistance of your own and other Neutral Governments whose interest should be as great as our own and whose losses have been far less. The problems of transport in Russia and of distribution can be solved only by the people of Russia themselves, with the assistance, advice, and supervision of your Commission.

Subject to such supervision, the problem of distribution should be solely under the control of the people of Russia themselves. The people in each locality should be given, as under the regime of the Belgian Relief Commission, the fullest opportunity to advise your Commission upon the methods and the personnel by which their community is to be relieved. In no other circumstances could it be believed that the purpose of this relief was humanitarian and not political, under no other conditions could it be certain that the hungry would be fed.

That such a course would involve cessation of all hostilities within definitive lines in the territory of Russia is obvious, and the cessation of hostilities would, necessarily, involve a complete suspension of the transfer of troops and military material of all sorts to and within Russian territory. Indeed, relief to Russia which did not mean a return to a state of peace would be futile, and would be impossible to consider.

Under such conditions as we have outlined, we believe

that your plan could be successfully carried into effect, and we should be prepared to give it our full support.

(*Signed*) V. E. ORLANDO
D. LLOYD GEORGE
WOODROW WILSON
G. CLEMENCEAU.

On the same day (April 17) that I received this reply I tried to send a wireless telegram to Moscow, addressed to M. Nikolai Lenin, in which I first repeated my letter to the Supreme Council, then its answer as quoted above, and ended with the following addition :

I would be glad to hear from you in this matter at your earliest convenience.

I may add that the neutral organisation which I propose offers its services in this cause without any remuneration whatever, but of course its expenditures in the purchase and transportation of supplies must be met by the Soviet Government.

Believe me, etc.
FRIDTJOF NANSEN.

It turned out, however, that there were unexpected difficulties in the way of sending this telegram to Russia. Although the four powerful members of the Supreme Council had agreed to the proposal to help Russia, several of their Governments refused to allow the big wireless-stations, which alone could transmit over such a long distance, to send off the information to Moscow, as they were not prepared to facilitate any communication with a Government which was not recognised. For a long time I tried in vain in every conceivable way to get the telegram dispatched.

Meanwhile, the Russian emigrants in Paris became extremely active in opposing this proposal, which they considered as a most dangerous obstacle to their policy. When I originally made my proposal I had several meetings with them to consider it ; and at that time they rightly felt that they ought not to oppose an attempt of that nature to carry relief to their necessitous countrymen. But gradually their attitude changed ; and in particular when the Supreme Council's reply laid down the condition that all hostilities in Russia must cease, they began to raise a vigorous agitation. Their view was that this condition would prevent Koltchak, who was then in East Russia with his army, from completing the work of marching on Moscow and liberating Russia from the sway of Bolshevism. They even delivered an official protest in the name of the "Russian Political Conference," signed by Prince Lvov, S. Sazonov, N. Tchaikowsky and B. Maklakoff.

It may be recalled that Soviet Russia was at that time being attacked by Koltchak's army in the east, and Denikin's army on the south ; and simultaneously Petlura's forces were fighting intermittently in Ukraine. Somewhat later came Yudenitch's offensive against Petrograd from the Baltic Provinces. The Russian emigrants in Paris were convinced that these attacks would attain their object and demolish the Soviet administration.

This view of the emigrants was not, however, shared in other quarters, where reliable information was available regarding the real state of affairs in Russia, and if the proposal detailed above met with opposition in the form of Koltchak refusing to suspend hostilities, the probability was that he would be compelled to do so by the Government's refusal to give him any such support as he had up to then enjoyed.

As it remained impossible to get the telegram sent to Moscow, and as, moreover, the Norwegian radio station was not yet ready to begin communicating with Russia, I telegraphed requesting the Norwegian Government for safety's sake to send a courier immediately to Russia with the telegram; but not even he succeeded in getting across the Russian frontier.

In my despair at being obliged to wait in uncertainty while the precious time slipped by, I returned from Paris to Norway intending, if necessary, to go to Russia myself with the telegram. Meanwhile, it had at last been safely got off by wireless from Berlin, and when I arrived in Norway I received the following reply by wireless telegram, signed by Tchitcherin:

SIR,

Your very kind message of April 17th containing your exchange of letters with the Council of Four reached us only on May 4th by way of the Nas wireless station and was at once given to the People's Commissariat of Social Welfare for thorough examination.

Wish in the name of the Russian Soviet Government to convey to you our heartiest thanks for the warm interest you manifest in the wellbeing of the Russian people. Great are indeed the sufferings and privations inflicted upon the Russian peoples by the inhuman blockade of the associated and so-called neutral Powers and by the incessant wars forced upon it against its will.

If left in peace and allowed free development Soviet Russia would soon be able to restore her national production, to regain her economic strength, to provide for her own needs, and to be helpful to other countries. But in the present situation in which she has been put by the inplacable policy of the associated Powers, help in foodstuffs from abroad would be most welcome to Russia, and the Russian Soviet Government appreciates most thankfully your humane and heartfelt response to her sufferings, and considering the universal respect surrounding your person will be especially glad to enter communication with you for the realisation of your scheme of help which you emphasize as being purely humanitarian.

On this basis of a humanitarian work of help to suffering people we would be pleased to do everything in our power to further the realisation of your project.

Unfortunately your benevolent intentions which you indicate yourself as being based upon purely humanitarian grounds and which according to your letter must be realised by a commission of fully non-political character, have been mixed up by others with political purposes. In the letter addressed to you by the four Powers your scheme is represented as involving cessation of hostilities and of transfer of troops and war materials and we regret very much that your original intentions have thus been fundamentally disfigured by the Governments of the associated Powers.

We need not explain to you that military operations which obviously have in view to change the external or internal condition of the involved countries belong wholly to the theme [? sphere] of politics and that likewise cessation of hostilities which are preventing the belligerent, who has every reason to expect successes, from obtaining them, is also a purely political act. Thus your sincerely charitable intention has been misused by others in order to cover such purposes, which are obviously political, with the semblance of an action originally humanitarian only.

Being ready to lend every assistance to your scheme so far as it bears the character you have ascribed to it in your letter, we at the same time do not wish to be the object of foul play, and knowing that you in the same [way] as ourselves mean business and wish really to attain the proposed, we would like to ask you whether this incantion [? inclusion] of heterogeneous purposes has been finally adopted by yourself.

We expect that we will be able to make it clear to you that, in order to realise your intentions, this intermission [? intromission] must be carefully avoided.

You are no doubt aware that the cessation of the wars forced upon the Russian people is likewise the object of our most warm desires; it must be known to you that we have many times proposed to the associated Governments to enter into negotiations in order to put an end to the present bloodshed and that we have even agreed to take part at the conference at Prinkipo notwithstanding the extremely unfavourable conditions proposed to us and also that we were the only party to accept it. We responded in the same peace-loving sense to overtures made by one of the Great Powers.

The Prinkipo conference was frustrated not by us but by our adversaries, the protegees of the associated Powers the counter-revolutionary Governments of Koltchak, Denikin and the others. These are the people with the help of which the Entente Governments are making war upon us and are endeavouring to obtain our destruction, and wherever they are victorious their victory means the triumph of the most extreme barbarity and bestiality, streams of blood and untold sufferings for the labouring masses, domination of the wildest reaction.

Koltchak from east, Denikin from the south, the Roumanian feudrie [?], the Polish and Finnish most reactionary militarists, the German barons, Teutonian white guards from the west, and Russian white guard bands from the north, these are the enemies whom the Entente Governments move against Soviet Russia and against whom as against Entente troops we are carrying on a desperate struggle with ever growing success.

The so-called Governments of Koltchak and Denikin are purely monarchical; all power belongs there to the wildest adherents of Tsarism, extreme Tsarist papers are in every way supported by them, Tsarist hymns are constantly sung, their ceremonies the so-called constitution of Koltchak are in reality monarchical, among their soldiers they distribute only Tsarist literature, under the domination of Denikin the adherents of the Constitutional Government of Russia are persecuted and under the domination of Koltchak the adherents of the Constituent Assembly are imprisoned or shot.

Pogrom waking [? making] literature is being widely distributed by these so-called Governments, and wherever Jews come under their domination they are the object of the most horrible bestialities. In the West, the Polish legionaries and the troops of the Ukrainian Counter-revolutionary Petlura, who are both supported and even directed by the Entente officers, have perpetrated such massacres of Jews, which by far surpasses the most horrible misdeeds of the Black Hundred of the old Tsarism. As the Russian Red Cross in its appeal to the International Red Cross on April 28th elaborately states whole villages, whole towns were burned in Russia, neither sex nor age was spared and in numerous places the whole Jewish population was literally wiped out by these troops, headed by Entente generals and officers.

The realm [? In the realm] of Koltchak and Denikin everything that was gained by the peasants through the revolution is being taken back from them. Koltchak declares solemnity [? solemnly in] manifestoes that peasants must not take possession [of] land again by force from the nobility, he orders in his decrees that the seizure of the land of the gentry by the peasants should be persecuted as a serious crime and crushes the resistance of the peasants by wholesale massacres, during which [in] some parts of Siberia many thousands of peasants were killed *en masse*.

For the worker this domination means every possible persecution, oppression, wholesale arrests and in many cases wholesale shootings, so that in some towns the workers were simply wiped out by the enraged ex-Tsarist officers, who are at the head of the Koltchak troops. The horrors perpetrated by these Koltchak officers defy description and their victims are innumerable, including all that is progressive, all that is free thinking [in] Siberia. Inebriated officers are torturing, flogging, tormenting in every way the unfortunate labouring population under their domination and to be a worker is to be predestined to be the object of their brutalities.

These are the adversaries against whom we are engaged in a desperate struggle and whom the associated Governments in every way support, providing them with war material, foodstuffs, financial help, military commanders, political advisers and on the north and east fronts sending their own troops to help them. In the hands of these barbarous bandits Entente rifles and Entente canons are sending death to the Russian workers and peasants struggling for their life and liberty.

The same Entente Governments are the real source of the military supplies, with the help of which our Polish, Roumanian, Finnish and other adversaries from the west are uninterruptedly attacking us and it was officially declared in the French Chamber of Deputies and in the British House of Commons that the policy of the Entente be now to send against Soviet Russia the armies of these nationalities.

An American radio of May 6th sent from Lyons says us most emphatically that the Entente announce [? encourages] the movement of the troops headed by the Russian counter-revolutionary general Yudenitch, which probably to attack Petrograd, that the Entente expects that the Bolsheviki will be forced to withdraw soon and that the associated Governments intend connection herewith to abinde [? abide, or accede] your plan of revictualling Russia.

While declaring that they have abandoned the idea of intervention the associated Governments are in reality carrying on the most reckless intervention policy and even the American Government, despite all the statements to the contrary published in the American press, seems at present wholly dominated by the deplorable hostility of the Clemenceau ministry against Soviet Russia.

This being the case, we are in a position to discuss cessation of hostilities only if we discuss the whole problem of our relations to our adversaries, that is in the first place to the associated Governments. That means to discuss peace and to open real negotiations bearing upon the true reasons of the war waged upon us and upon those conditions that can bring us lasting peace.

We are always ready to enter into peace negotiations and we are ready to do it now as before, and we will be glad to begin discussing these questions, but of course directly with the other belligerents, that is with the associated Governments or else with the persons empowered by the latter. But it is of course impossible to us to make any concessions referring to these fundamental problems of our existence under the disguise of a presumably humanitarian work. This latter must remain purely humanitarian and non-political and we will welcome every proposal from your side made to us in the spirit of your letter sent by you to the Council of Four on April 3rd. To these wholly non-political proposals we respond most gladly.

We thank you most heartily for your good intentions, we are ready to give you every possibility of controlling the realisation of such humanitarian scheme, we will of course cover all the expenses of this work and the costs of the foodstuffs and can pay, if you desire, by Russian goods. But seeing that your original plan has been so unfortunately discontinued [? disfigured] and considering that the most complex and difficult questions this created must first be thoroughly elucidated, we suggest that you take the necessary steps to enable delegates of our Government to meet you and your collaborators abroad and to discuss these questions, and we ask you kindly to indicate the time and the place for this conference between our delegates and the leaders of your commission and what guarantee can be obtained for the free passage of our delegates through countries influenced by the Entente.

People's Commissary for Foreign Affairs,
TCHITCHERIN.

I at once telegraphed this telegram to Paris, where it had probably already been picked up by the wireless-station. I also telegraphed to Tchitcherin in Moscow that I was prepared to go to Moscow to negotiate, if that should prove desirable, but that I must first learn the attitude of the allied Governments to the Soviet Government's reply.

As there was no prospect of inducing the Supreme Council to drop their condition that hostilities must cease, the whole project had to be abandoned for the time being.

In my opinion, however, this was regrettable. I am convinced that if these negotiations had attained their object the state of affairs in Europe would have been entirely different from what we see to-day. The raising of the blockade, and Russia's renewed entry into relations with the outside world on a purely economic basis at a time when she still possessed considerable supplies of raw materials, would unavoidably have exerted a great influence on the restoration of the equilibrium of European production and consumption.

Alike in 1919 and 1920 Russia was, in reality, only considered from the political standpoint, and this interest chiefly took the form of support, sometimes of a powerful nature, rendered to the attacks made on the Soviet republic by Koltchak, Denikin, Yudenitch, the Polish offensive and Wrangel.

Great Britain was occupied in safeguarding the East against Bolshevik propaganda and in securing a firm position in the Baltic by favouring the Baltic group of buffer-States.

France founded her whole policy *vis-à-vis* Russia on her friendship with the Russia of the old regime.

Germany was pursuing, in a spirit half political, half commercial, her sole possibility of free development, namely towards the East.

It was in 1921 that people in the west of Europe became strongly attracted by the possibilities of fruitful operations which they thought they could secure by resuming commercial relations with Russia. That was the time when commercial treaties were concluded with Great Britain and with Germany, when the provisional trade agreement with Italy was signed, and when the discussions were carried on with the American senators Goodrich and France.

Even though the negotiations had the advantage of transferring the consideration of the Russian problem from the political to the economic sphere, it cannot be denied that the exaggerated expectations which had been formed were disappointed, at any rate to a large extent.

Compared with the figures for trade before the war, the genuine transactions were still rather modest, and one feels that they have a somewhat artificial character. The ordinary balance of imports and exports shows that in 1921 Russia purchased foreign products to a value of 248 million gold roubles, while she only sold to a value of 20 millions (compared with exports in 1913 worth 1,520 millions and imports worth 1,375 millions). The position improved somewhat in 1922, when the value of exports rose to about 80 million gold roubles, while that of imports amounted to 500 millions. But the abnormal economic nature of the transactions is still very noticeable.

The commercial treaty with Great Britain has undoubtedly made possible quite an important amount of trade, but really serious and lasting connections do not seem to have been established.

In the case of Germany, a quite considerable business connection was developed; but it is significant that in all transactions with Russian buyers the German merchants demand cash payment. Notwithstanding the fact that Russia, in the first nine months of 1921, bought German goods to the value of 33 million gold roubles, and in the corresponding period of 1922 to the value of 102 millions, the German commercial houses have not opened any credit worth mentioning for the Russians.

This unfortunate result is to a large extent due, no doubt, to a sense of the impermanency of the Russian market; its purchasing-power appears to lack a sound foundation. Moreover, there is no denying that the circumstance that all business was done through the clumsy machinery of the Vnesjtorg (i.e. the Commissariat for Foreign Trade) was not calculated to increase the confidence of foreign capital.

The Governments and the business world also found their attitude towards Russia much affected and complicated by the famine, of unparalleled severity, which devastated Russia after the harvest of 1921 had failed in the most fertile regions, especially in the Volga districts and in Southern Ukraine.

After the International Conference at Geneva, which opened on August 15, 1921, and was composed of delegates from forty-eight Red Cross and philanthropic associations and twelve Governments, had requested me to put myself at the head of the relief work for famine-stricken Russia, I made an agreement in Moscow on

August 27th with Tchitcherin, as representative of the Soviet Government, concerning the method of providing relief for the starving Russian people and the raising of an international State loan for that purpose, under full control of a neutral organisation and the Governments of the Great Powers, who would guarantee that the loan was exclusively and impartially used to combat the famine.

But at the Assembly of the League of Nations in Geneva in September, 1921, I tried in vain to induce the League to assume the lead in this relief work, and to raise an international governmental loan for the purpose of helping the starving millions of Russia, who might yet be saved if relief were brought to them immediately, before winter made transport difficult, but who were otherwise doomed to die.

There was superabundance of food, transport, and workmen in the world. The maize was used as fuel in the locomotives of Argentina, the ships lay idle in many countries, and thousands of men were unemployed. Some of the idle ships, with a small part of the unemployed men, could easily carry sufficient superfluous American corn to save the starving and dying millions.

The refusal of the League of Nations to take up this work was due to several different reasons. Some considered it difficult to ask the Governments of the Western Powers, already so deeply plunged in debt, to give a loan to a Government which was not even recognised, and where the security was regarded as being of doubtful value; and moreover, the unemployment in several of the countries was so menacing that it was thought that the money would be needed at home.

Another objection—and one which undoubtedly carried much weight in the minds of many of the politicians—was that which the Russian emigrants in particular advanced, namely that to relieve the starving and suffering Russian people would be tantamount to supporting the Soviet Government and the Bolsheviks, and that such action would be indefensible. Many of the emigrants confessed frankly that they would rather sacrifice all these millions of their countrymen, and leave guiltless men, women and children to a certain and cruel death, than contemplate the possibility of the Bolshevik Government receiving any kind of help.

In my opinion it is a matter for sincere regret that it proved impossible to grant the loan we asked for. If the necessary money had been forthcoming then—in September—there would still have been time to get supplies to the stricken districts in Russia. The starving millions of peasants and their farm stock could have been saved, and Russian agriculture raised again to prosperity. The export of corn, and therewith the country's purchasing-power, could have been restored, at any rate to a large extent.

Russia, as a factor in the economic life of Europe, would in that case have been something very different from what she is now, and Europe would have been the better off in consequence. As it is, Russia's economic condition has been radically made worse by the famine, her agriculture has been subjected to a great set-back over large areas, and those the most fertile, and it will be a great work to restore what has been destroyed, not to mention all the needless and indescribable suffering which could have been avoided and the millions of lives needlessly lost. The hearts of politicians are often hard and inhuman.

Meanwhile, the course that events thus took also helped to weaken the faith of the business world in Russia's economic capacity.

The unsuccessful conference at Genoa, in the spring of 1922, the failure to ratify the commercial treaty with Italy which was signed by M. Tchitcherin and M. Krassin, and finally the failure to ratify the agreement arrived at between M. Krassin and Mr. Leslie Urquhart—all this made a very unfavourable impression on all those who had hoped immediately and to a large extent to be able to resume profitable business relations with Russia.

As a matter of fact the political interest in Russia is once more gaining ground. To prevent the Rapallo Treaty from leading to a more intimate entente between Germany and the Soviet Government, the idea of a Franco-Russian *rapprochement* has been taken up in certain French circles ; and there has even been talk of a possible resuscitation of the old Treaty of Alliance.

It is also symptomatic of European opinion at

this moment, that even countries which have pursued such a cautious and reserved policy towards Russia as Denmark, have now begun negotiations with at least the object of arriving at a commercial agreement.[1]

I do not believe that the Russian people take any serious interest in the political quarrels which split up Europe. My impression is that Russia does not see anything more in the possibility actually offered of resuming closer relations with the outside world than a means to obtain foreign co-operation in the great work of reconstruction which it has to carry through.

It is important in establishing this contact that both the foreign countries and Russia herself should adopt the European economic point of view of which I have spoken.

It is also of the utmost importance that both sides should endeavour to understand each other and try to gain an objective knowledge of each other.

The aim of the succeeding chapters must accordingly be to restore the economic interest in Russia on a sound foundation: that is, on an impartial recognition of the real state of the country.

If we study the Russian problem with minds free from preconceived opinions, whether pessimistic or optimistic, we shall find it less hard to discover a solution which will help to restore the international economic equilibrium, and in so doing render it considerably easier to secure peace.

[1] Since the above was written an agreement has been arrived at, and has been accepted by both parties.

CHAPTER III

THE GENERAL DEVELOPMENT OF RUSSIA'S ECONOMIC ORGANISATION

WHETHER or not one strongly disagrees with the present administration of Russia, it must at any rate be admitted that the way in which Russian conditions generally are discussed in a large section of the Press in West Europe betrays, on the whole, little understanding, or what is worse, little desire to understand.

When one endeavours to form an objective opinion about what is happening in Russia, one presumably ought first and foremost to secure reliable information about it, and not to depend on mere idle rumours. Moreover, one ought not to forget that the present administration is founded on a revolution, and that after all revolutionary methods in most countries are less lenient than those of ordinary peace-time. One may, perhaps, condemn on good grounds all revolutions, as being an unreliable and too expensive method of reforming the community ; but we should bear in mind that the contemporary organisation of Society in a very considerable number of the States of Europe—France, Germany, Italy, Hungary, Portugal, and Greece, merely to mention some of them—has been built up on revolutions. And if we once admit their moral justification—not least in a country like Russia, where the people had practically no political franchise—it is arbitrary to maintain that some revolutions, such as that in 1905 or the Duma-revolution in March, 1917, with Kerenski later on as its leader, were justifiable because one agreed more or less with these people, while on the contrary the Bolshevik revolution was a crime committed by bandits and murderers with whom we do not agree.

Even if, in the strongest terms, we condemn persecution and cruelties inflicted on those who hold different opinions, as being utterly atrocious, we must also in all fairness remember that the Russian people has been inured to this throughout its whole history, and that cruelties and political persecution were not unknown under the old administration of Russia. Consider the hundreds and thousands of imprisonments and cases of ill-treatment of political opponents—not only in Finland and Poland, but also in Russia itself; consider the misdeeds of the Black Hundred under Tsarism; think of the banishments to Siberia without trial, not to mention the persecution of the Jews, the "pogroms," when thousands of innocent Jews were killed, and which were sometimes even set on foot when the authorities desired to divert attention from other irregularities.

No, the Russian people has been through a severe school; it is accustomed to ill-treatment.

It should also be remembered that a number of those who are now its rulers spent years of their lives in prison and exile.

It is said that the present Government of Russia is an oligarchy, only representative of a single class. But the old Government was surely an oligarchy to a still higher degree, representative of a still smaller part of the Russian people. And surely the oppression of the other classes was bad in those days too, only that centuries had habituated them to it.

This difference should also be borne in mind, that whereas the former ruling class had nothing to avenge—for it had always had the upper hand—the class which is ruling now has much to avenge in the way of oppression and partly also of extortion, throughout a long period. And to these formerly oppressed classes we must add the Jews, who have always been hated, persecuted and inhumanly treated in Russia. Just think of the law which forbade Jews to live in the capital of the Empire; not to speak of the persecutions. Is it strange that all this bred more hate, and that the persecuted race joined in the revolution when the opportunity came? We know that there is—sometimes, at any rate—a nemesis in history, and that the present must often suffer for the sins of the past.

I think that one ought to remember all this before pronouncing judgment on what is going on in Russia now. Here, as ever, the old saying applies, that *tout comprendre, c'est tout pardonner.*

The more I consider the position in Russia at the outset of the revolution, the more I become convinced that the establishment of a moderate, constitutional administration was psychologically impossible.

From extreme reactionary Tsarism before 1917 on the right hand, physical necessity made the pendulum swing across to the extreme left—to Communism and the "Dictatorship of the Proletariat."

When the Press of Western Europe, in its righteous zeal to maintain the only saving doctrine, is so morally shocked at Bolshevism in Russia, which it regards as a poisonous and disintegrating social pest, engendered in malice and nourished by criminal rapacity and class hatred, it is only right to point out, on the one hand, that we are not justified in calling any organisation of the community the only good and perfect one, any more than we can call the others a total failure. None are entirely without good features ; the question is, therefore, which possesses most.

On the other hand, it is a fact that Bolshevism has passed through so many phases in its evolution that it is indeed no easy task to say what Bolshevism really is now. I must admit that I, at least, cannot undertake this, although I have spent considerable time in trying to penetrate the mystery.

From the point of view of history it is interesting to study the Communist theorists who between 1917 and 1921 laid down the principles which ought to guide the Soviet Republic. But I do not think that all this literature will help us much to understand present-day Russia and what Bolshevism really is at this moment, for the practical application of genuine Communism is now extremely rare.

It appears to me that the kernel of the teaching of Bolshevism must—at any rate at first—have been the assertion of *work* as the only thing which justified a place in and right to enjoy the advantages of the community; and it denied every advantage conferred by birth and inheritance.

For work is necessary—at any rate in these latitudes—in order to extort from our soil what we need to sustain life. It is, therefore, and must be unjust, that some should live as parasites on the community without working, while others have to work far too much. This inequitable distribution was not least flagrant in Russia.

No doubt there was a tendency there, at an earlier date, rather to look down upon work, especially manual work, as something only fit for a lower caste. Of course this is partly a survival from the days of slavery which has persisted not merely in Russia, but also to a certain extent in other countries: manual labour was left to serfs; it was not for free men.

That this social view of work aroused a violent reaction as soon as the workmen got their chance, is not unnatural, and that they chiefly thought of work as being manual work is also comprehensible. The Russian people had now to be taught to respect work to the full.

I must confess that I do not share the indignation many feel at a number of the ways in which this was done ; for instance, that men and women of the different classes were forced to do public work once a week, and that even ladies of the upper class and aristocracy, who had not been accustomed to any kind of work previously, had every Saturday to join in cleaning railway stations or scrubbing other public buildings. It even appears to be wholesome in many ways for members of all classes in the community to learn together the need of work, provided, of course, that they are not taken away from more important work, or that health and age do not stand in the way.

One outcome of a conviction of the importance of work was the arrangement by which the affairs of the municipalities were to be administered by local soviets, or councils, composed of representatives of the different categories of work.

That the manual worker, or labour-proletariat, was taken as the centre of gravity, while the recognition of the value of brain-work was less clear, at any rate, at the outset, was natural enough in view of what has been said above.

It represented a not altogether unreasonable reaction against the earlier tyranny of the so-called upper class. What was wanted was to give due emphasis to the new way, and this led to the catch-word " Dictatorship of the Proletariat," driving home the protest against the old.

But not only the so-called intellectuals, meaning

chiefly the upper class, but also *capital* was marked down. It was held that capital, which should of course be saved-up work, exerts an immoral effect by giving its possessors advantages which are unfair and harmful to the community. Thus we have the glaring injustice that through the amassing of wealth by one man's work or even by a single lucky speculation, not only he and his family, but his children and even descendants for several generations can live without working, as parasites on the community, while others work for them. Speculation itself is essentially immoral and calculated to secure advantages from other people's work without working oneself. And it is worse still, when the parasites waste the fruits of other men's work outside the country.

A violent protest from below against this incongruity is easy to understand.

The attack was aimed at the *money-system*, which was a means of amassing capital, and which, by its payment of interest, makes it possible for parasites to exist without working. Money ought preferably to be abolished—they overlooked the important fact that the economic life of the community, during thousands of years' development, has been based on money as the necessary medium of exchange.

Now it was thought that this basis could be torn away with a single wrench, and that a return could be made to the primitive state when money was unknown. The attack was also aimed at the *right of ownership itself*. By the ownership of property, and still more by hiring it out, a man could live without working. All property, houses, woods, land, mines, etc., were therefore nationalised.

Free trade had also to be abolished. It created a class of middlemen, who were considered superfluous. The shops were closed. All trade, except in certain products, was forbidden. The necessaries of life would be distributed by the State.

On the whole it must be said that the Communist theories professed by the revolutionary Bolsheviks of 1917 have pre-eminently had negative results: the dissolution of the old army, the disturbance of social conditions, etc., etc.

In their attempted practical application they led to the formation of economic organisms which were so artificial, and which acted so inefficiently, that they could only be kept going for some years at the cost of enormous sacrifices.

The nationalised undertakings, such as banks, transport, factories, mines, municipal agriculture, and warehouses, were combined into enormous organisations which worked for the account of the the State, and which were meant to provide everything necessary for the people.

Not only could the clumsy machinery thus created not satisfy the consumers' most necessary requirements, except in an extremely inadequate way, but it was solely by help of the old stocks of all sorts which existed that this could be done at all for a short time. These supplies were exhausted after a few years, and then a change of system became inevitable.

From first to last it was a vast experiment made on the whole Russian population. It might seem that as regards especially the Russian peasant population, forming the great majority of the Russian people, the Communist idea was not unfamiliar, since the land in the Russian village (the *mir*) belongs, according to ancient custom, to the village, not to the individual peasants.

All the same, it soon appeared that the whole system was impracticable, and that the experiment could not possibly succeed. In the domain of agriculture, which is, of course, the decisive and all-dominating means of livelihood in Russia, Communism was in reality never tried. The few experiments made with Communist agriculture came completely to grief.

The houses in the towns, having no owners interested in keeping them in repair, quickly fell into dilapidation ; industry, without owners or specially interested directors, declined disastrously, and so on. And, meanwhile, the State's employees increased to veritable armies, who had to be supported by the State. The whole thing threatened to collapse.

Soon the leaders themselves saw that it would not work, and "the new economic policy" (the well-known N.E.P.) was inaugurated in the spring of 1921, for the simple reason that there were no longer means in the country to keep the Communist experiment going.

They recognised—as it was said—that the community was not yet ripe for the Communist form of administration, and they were compelled to return, more or less, to capitalist methods.

It was, above all, under pressure of the great mass of the peasantry that the rigid and artificial economic mould, into which the orthodox Communists tried to squeeze the life of Russia, finally burst.

It was the just demands of the agricultural labourers (and not the efforts of the old *bourgeoisie*) which occasioned the mighty movement for denationalisation and for a normal economic structure, which will be the salvation of Russia.

In reality, it was the peasant who suffered most under the regime which was suffocating the Russian nation. Forced to give up to the State his whole crop, except what was considered strictly necessary to support himself and his family, he had a right, according to Communist principles, to obtain the articles of clothing he required, and to enjoy gratis all the advantages and services of the State.

But as he really got nothing, or hardly anything, he demanded more and more loudly that he should have the right to dispose of the produce of his labour himself, after paying the taxes and other dues.

To give the peasant the right to sell, though it be only part of his produce—would not that open a dangerous breach in the Communistic edifice? I am convinced that it is not so much the socialising of production, as the turning of the whole machinery of distribution into a State institution, that is the hall-mark of true Communism.

The end of it was that requisitioning of the

peasants' produce was given up, and instead a tax in kind was imposed, consisting mainly of corn; and for the rest the peasant was given the right to sell his produce as he liked within the country.

The immediate result of this alteration was, of course, that the home trade had to be liberated, first the retail trade, and then the general economic intercourse, which is so important that it led to the creation of the whole financial organisation which I shall describe in a later chapter.

This was all the more significant, since the Soviet Government had tried, in accordance with Communist principles, completely to suppress the money system, as mentioned above.

The resuscitation of trade brought with it a circulation and distribution of goods which was certainly rather modest when we think of the statistics from before the war, but which was otherwise quite remarkable. Meanwhile, the Government found it continually more difficult to cover the deficit on the State's production.

When it was seen that the moment was approaching when transport and industry and the State's machinery for distribution would have used up all the supplies and emptied the State treasury, an attempt was made to escape bankruptcy by taking advantage of this new stream of life.

While they continued to be the State's official purveyors, supplying the needs of the Army and the needs of a part of the people, the productive undertakings and public services had themselves to obtain part of what they needed by accepting payment from the public who received the advantages of their work.

The railways, tramways, water transport, and electric services organised themselves (or tried to organise themselves) on a commercial basis ; the factories were grouped in trusts, and sold their products through Co-operative Societies and private stores, in order themselves and at their own expense to arrange for the supply and utilisation of raw-stuffs.

Under the Communist regime a factory got its raw materials from the State ; it did not pay its workmen, as they received their " pajok " (Government ration of food), and cards which gave them access to the Government stores to procure such clothes, boots, etc., as they had a right to. On the other hand, the factory had to hand over its whole production to the State.

Since the introduction of the " new economic policy " everything has to be paid for.

Every undertaking must have its own budget, and its income and expenditure must balance ; for the Soviet Government has come to the end of its gold reserves and cannot contribute to other economic organisations than those which are absolutely indispensable for the life of the State. Those undertakings which show a deficit run the risk of being hired out to private owners, given under a concession to foreigners, or simply closed.

In reality, it is impossible to describe in a few words Russia's economic organisation, because several types of organisation exist simultaneously.

The Communist system continues, I suppose, to have a theoretical existence in the minds of the leaders, but in practice they have passed over to State Socialism, as we have seen, and then to a regime wherein private initiative constantly receives a larger share. The Co-operatives, besides, play a very important rôle.

In later chapters on transport, industry, trade, etc., I shall try to illustrate and give concrete examples to show the truth of these general impressions.

Under life's pressure the whole Russian organisation must develop, and even if the general position is still extremely difficult, one can already see encouraging results.

During the deliberations I had early this year with the leaders of the various departments of Russian economic life I was able to observe the serious and methodical way in which they were trying, by strenuous efforts, to carry out their economic reconstruction based on the principles of the new economic policy.

Even the caution with which they advance is really a reason for believing that their work will succeed. They have given up trying to settle by orders of the day the thousand problems raised daily by practical life.

They have a full understanding of the complexity of the economic phenomena and of the dangers which lie in the constant interference by the State in the life of industry, trade and agriculture.

At the end of a report on the results of the new

economic policy just published by the Supreme Council of National Economy, the Industrial Commission states that, in its opinion, the number of trusts is too large, and one notes a tendency to greater industrial concentration. But, it is added, "None the less it would be irrational to hurry by administrative measures this natural development, and it is better to wait till the change comes by itself."

Well, this is language one is not used to hearing from Soviet Russia.

CHAPTER IV

RUSSIA'S TRANSPORT SERVICES

IF normal economic relations between Europe and Russia are to be restored, the first condition must be that the countries concerned possess technical apparatus capable of transporting the products of exchange.

In what state, then, are the Russian communications by water and land?

The inland transport by river, canal and lake has in recent years been equal to about a quarter of what it was before the war. For 1913 it was about 37 million tons, and for six months of 1922 only 4·3 millions. This reduction is due in part to the circumstance that the inland fleet stands very greatly in need of repair, and in part to the fact that trade in Russia itself has dwindled so much.

According to a report which I have just received from my representative in Astrakhan, the traffic on the Volga and Kama has been quite considerable, notwithstanding all the difficulties that have had to be overcome. In the course of 1922 there were shipped from Astrakhan three million tons of goods, chiefly crude oil.

By way of comparison between the state of things before the war and now, it may be of interest to give the following statistics of the number of ships belonging to various companies which have been plying on the Volga and Kama, in the Astrakhan Government :

	Pre-War.	1922.	Probable No. in 1923.
Passenger boats in use ..	388	186	86
Passenger boats in reserve ..	—	—	35
Tugs in use	300	150	60
Tugs in disrepair	200	160	80

The restoration of inland navigation to full working order would exercise a great influence on the general economic condition of the country; but it would demand a large expenditure of capital.

As regards maritime transport, Russia, as we know, lost the greater part of her mercantile marine during her foreign and civil wars. There is consequently a great shortage of ships, and in 1921 and 1922 Russia was obliged to charter foreign tonnage at high prices.

The Soviet Government has made great efforts to improve the harbours, which were partially destroyed or damaged during the war and the revolution.

Important export harbours had been lost. Reval had gone to Esthonia, and Riga, Libau and Windau had gone to Latvia. Russia has done strenuous work in improving the ports of Petrograd, Novorossisk, Odessa, and several lesser ports in the Black Sea.

In the course of its work since the autumn of

1921 in the fight against the famine, our organisation has constantly used the Russian harbours for the transport of our goods, and I have received regular reports from our technical representatives on the spot.

They have been surprised at the rapidity with which many repairs were carried out in spite of great difficulties.

Novorossisk, for instance, which had been bombarded by the Turks in 1914, and where some of the warehouses had been burnt down in 1920, was largely repaired. Its stone quays have now been restored, whereas the wooden quays, which are of greater extent, have still not been put right. The fixed and floating cranes and several of the huge corn elevators are working, and the personnel is to a large extent the same as before the war.

In the summer of 1922 the imports to the port of Petrograd totalled 900,000 tons of goods, and the exports 300,000 tons. This represents 22 per cent. of the goods in transit via this port in 1913.

It is well known what an influence it has always had on Russia's foreign policy that the country has no other important exits than those through two locked seas, the Baltic and Black Sea, to which others hold the keys. Russian exports and imports can therefore be smothered at any time, and this permanent dependence upon the course of foreign politics fosters a continual feeling of insecurity in Russia.

Here again I believe that by establishing a

regular economic connection between the various countries of Europe one would lay a far more solid foundation and obtain far better securities for peace than by political conventions, however advantageous their terms might be.

The immediate result of the gratis system, which was to be introduced in all the public services, was that the railways were inundated by hordes of soldiers, prisoners and refugees, who got themselves transported free from one end of Russia to the other after Brest-Litovsk. This unchecked migration, the political and social disturbances of all kinds, the formation of local soviets of railwaymen with their own elected railway commissaries, who acted more or less according to their own sweet will, the devastation wrought by the civil war and by the advances and retreats of the armies, and added to that the greater and greater shortage of fuel—all these factors in combination completely overwhelmed the system of transport.

The only means to get the railways under control again was to place them entirely under military management. Under Trotzky's dictatorship an immense effort was made to restore a little order and to repair the ruined railways. The improvement of the railways was regarded as one of the most important strategical points in the "labour front," and it was just as good to employ the Red Army on it as to conscript other people for forced labour.

In spite of all efforts, however, Trotzky's energetic labour campaign did not succeed entirely; the difficulties remained in part invincible.

Under the administration of Dzershinsky, appointed "Commissary for Roads and Communications," the whole system of transport was reorganised in 1921, at the same time that the "New Economic Policy" was introduced.

The Communistic gratis-system was abolished; the administration of the various lines was handed over to committees who were given a certain amount of independence, and who were permitted to organise their railways on a commercial basis.

This complete readjustment, introduced at a moment when Russia was economically exhausted, and in addition was stricken by a famine more terrible than any that had gone before, could not, of course, be carried out without great difficulty.

Nevertheless, it brought about a considerable improvement in the working of the whole system of transport, an improvement of which I have been able to convince myself by the numerous reports from our delegates who have had to superintend the transport of the food-stuffs despatched to the starving populations of the Volga and the Ukraine.

In addition to this radical readjustment of the system itself, energetic measures were taken to improve the lines and bridges.

Thus it may be mentioned that by August 1, 1922, 1,542 bridges had been completely repaired; 2,090 bridges had been temporarily put right; while only 40 still remained in disrepair.

At the same time a considerable amount of worn-out railway material had been replaced, and all the lines had been rendered fit for traffic. It is hoped that by 1926 the work of improving the whole railway system will be finished.

Anyone who travelled in Russia in 1919, 1920, or 1921, and who travels over the same ground to-day, is struck by the remarkable results that have been achieved by the dreaded, but energetic and methodical, Commissary of Traffic.

[It will be remembered that Dzershinsky was president of the much feared Tsjeka, or revolutionary police.]

I am not now thinking of the fairly fast passenger trains with sleeping and restaurant cars, which were put on again on the main lines (Petrograd-Moscow, Kharkov-Crimea or Tiflis, etc.), for the number of people who gain by this is pretty limited; but I am thinking of the change which may be observed in the whole administration of the railways and of the orderliness and regular work which have replaced the dangerous anarchy at the beginning of the revolution and the disorganisation of 1920 and 1921.

I had an interesting conversation with Dzershinsky about the transport problem.

The Russian railways [he said] are quite on a level with the genuine requirements, and are capable of carrying all the goods that Russian and foreign consignors can send by them. The proof that the circulation is normal and can easily be speeded up if the quantity of goods in transit increases is that we have a reserve of 3,000 locomotives in perfect order and of about 60,000 goods wagons.

Our capacity to repair the material made great strides during the last months of 1922. In July of that year 65 per cent. of the locomotive-park was out of order; in December this percentage had fallen to 56 per cent. This means that not only have the repairs been able to cover the current needs, but that we have also repaired reserve material which was in an unusable state. As regards the wagons, the position is more difficult. But none the less the monthly deficiency will be almost covered by the repairs.

The Russian railways actually transport at the present time a quantity of goods equivalent to 30 per cent. of the quantity transported before the war. Technically speaking, they would be capable of transporting twice as much: on some lines the goods in transit reached 60 per cent. or 70 per cent. of the amount in 1913.

If the Russian railways still show a large financial deficit despite the efforts we are making to reduce the working expenses, this is due to the much too small quantity of goods that we have to transport. Our tariffs, even if they are very high for the Russian home market, are nevertheless lower according to the gold standard than they were before the war. And, above all, if we raise them, the amount of transport will decline and our receipts will not rise.

Thus the working of the railways can only become financially normal in proportion to the rise of the general economic level.

The greatest difficulty we have to meet is the insufficiency of our supplies of fuel—coal, wood, and petroleum. For lack of working capital we cannot secure sufficient supplies in time; for, in accordance with the new economic policy, we are obliged to pay, for instance, for our wood, which the State previously procured gratis for the railways by means of forced labour imposed upon the peasants. With the shortage of horses it is also difficult to bring the fuel to the railways.

According to Dzershinsky's statements, therefore, the position of Russian transport is far from being as catastrophic as the European Press likes to represent it as being. The vast technical apparatus which connects Archangel with the Crimea, and Odessa with Tashkend and Vladivostok, is working on a reduced scale, but it is being kept in order, and with the advent of increased economic activity it can augment its services.

Russia is a convalescent, her life is still that of a patient. As the wounded organs heal and begin to act normally the blood will again begin to circulate more rapidly in her veins.

There was one special direction in which Dzershinsky said that his department wished for a regular connection with foreign countries. The Russian technique of transport is rather far behind the technique of America and Western Europe. The Commissariat for the System of Communications would therefore very much like to send engineers abroad to study the transport problem. "Unfortunately," said Dzershinsky, "this plan has hitherto not been realised to any extent, on account of the difficulties raised against the entry of Russians into the countries which interest us."

I believe steps have already been taken to carry out this plan, and I do not doubt that the result will be excellent both for Russia and for the countries which agree to co-operate with the Russian engineers in this purely technical and economic field.

In spite of the great difficulties that the railway administration has had to combat on account of lack of credit, Dzershinsky is nevertheless personally against allowing foreign capital to take a direct share in the Russian system of communications.

His real opinion is that an increase of the activities of the railways must follow upon the development of agriculture and industry, and correspond to the progressive increase of the goods to be transported. The credit allowed to certain lines would, in his view, be paid back in two years. But such financing ought to be arranged through the medium of the Russian State, whose various economic councils prepare and direct the general work of reconstruction in the various districts.

It seems to me rather unlikely that foreign capital will give the Russian State credit destined for the railways without having any share in organising and controlling its utilisation. It appears to me that the only way to help the Russian railways to surmount the really difficult period would be to give short-term credit to certain railways of special interest, the repair or rapid development of which would be a decisive factor in increasing production or improving the distribution of produce.

By helping on to their feet certain systems of lines in the Archangel region, for instance, one would render possible a better exploitation of the forests; by restoring quicker communications with Siberia one would make it possible to develop again the butter industry which was so flourishing before the war and which had been developed in the course of a few years. The production of corn could be encouraged in the Kuban region, and similarly the production of sugar and corn in northern Ukraine, by making the rapid distribution of the produce possible through better transport facilities.

It goes without saying that an improvement of transport facilities which induced an increase of local production would react favourably on the financial position of the whole railway system.

According to a report that Bogdanov, president of the Supreme Council of National Economy, kindly sent me, the Russian railways of the third rate of importance run at a loss, and their working must be expected to give a deficit of 29 million gold roubles in 1923. The desirability of closing them for three years has therefore been discussed, but has been abandoned after calculation that not only would the resumption of work cost nearly 85 million gold roubles, but also that the income of the railways of the first and second class would fall to the extent of nearly 12 million gold roubles a year if their goods traffic was deprived of the supplies passing over the third class lines.

Every increase, therefore, in the quantity of goods transported in Russia really entails a reduction of the railways' deficit, for the railway organism costs less when it is working at full power.

I must add that though I was struck by Dzershinsky's logic and sense for the practical, but though his efforts to organise the transport system on a purely commercial basis appeared to proceed from a very sound (and not at all "State") appreciation of the economic circumstances, I cannot entirely share his opinion of the real condition of the Russian transport system.

According to what he says, it would almost seem as if the railways, which he has succeeded in raising from the dreadful condition of chaos into which they had sunk, were really an organism in splendid condition and development, going, indeed, at "reduced speed," but only because Russia's economic life has not grown equally rapidly and has not been able to contribute the quantity of goods required in order to set them going at full speed.

In reality the Russian transport system still works rather slowly and rather badly.

I have not received any personal impression of this, as the Russian Government, with the most perfect Russian hospitality, placed the finest saloon-cars at my disposal on my journeys in 1921, 1922 and 1923.

I cannot even say that our delegates in the famine relief work have suffered overmuch under the transport difficulties, except in the spring of 1922 when, *inter alia*, they went from Samara to Moscow by a train which was three weeks late. They have, moreover, enjoyed facilities and diplomatic privileges secured by the agreement that I concluded with Tchitcherin before the relief work began. Similarly our goods transports have always enjoyed special privileges: gratis carriage, priority, protection of the sealed wagons by soldiers of the Red Army, etc.

It is from the reports themselves, sent to me by the various organs of the Soviet Government, that I have convinced myself that if the development of the Russian transport system is delayed by the insufficiency of production, the development of production in turn is also seriously delayed by the insufficiency of transport.

I note with pleasure the fact that the percentage of locomotives under repair declined between July and December, 1922, from 65 per cent. to 56 per cent. But seeing that the Commissariat for Foreign Trade has recently purchased in Germany and Sweden 1,200 locomotives, of which nearly 1,000 were delivered in December, 1922, the percentage of engines in disrepair can easily have been reduced without the repair shops having made corresponding progress.

On the whole one must not forget that when the state of the Russian railways has improved, it is not an unimportant consideration that the Russian Government bought locomotives, rails and tenders, etc., at a cost of 24 million pounds sterling, through the railway mission headed by Professor Lomonosov, which they sent abroad. I do not think that the actual condition of the Russian finances will allow a repetition of this measure, of which I would be the first to admit the wisdom.

According to Bogdanov's report, 45 per cent. to 50 per cent. of the railway line sleepers have grown so old that they ought to be changed.

According to the plan which has just been adopted, 22 million sleepers ought to be removed annually in order to avert the crisis.

The Soviet Press declared as far back as November, 1921, that 43 million sleepers ought to be changed, 19 million of these immediately. However, it was not possible to change more than

8·5 million in 1922, and most of the new ones could not be impregnated. (The number of sleepers impregnated in the State factories was only 100,000 in 1919, but it rose in 1920 to 293,000, in 1921 to 423,000, and in 1922 to 940,000.)

Even though the station outfits, signal-wires and poles, which were in a bad state in 1920, were largely improved, the rails of the lighter type were a good deal worn, and compelled the trains to run at reduced speed.

Despite the efforts to make the working as economical as was at all possible, there was two and a half times as much fuel used per kilometre in 1922 as in 1912. It is true that the output of work by the very badly paid personnel has increased in comparison with 1921, but it has not risen to even one-half of what it was before the war. And if we put the quantity of goods transported in 1913 at 100, the quantity transported since 1919 does not exceed the following percentages: in 1919 = 17 per cent.; in 1920 = 20 per cent.; in 1921 and 1922 = 22 per cent.

Finally there is a very important difficulty of which Dzershinsky is very well aware, and which he has energetically fought against ever since 1920, but which he is unfortunately very far from having got in hand. This is the theft which goes on on a vast scale during the railway transport of the goods.

I must here, however, interpolate the remark that of the goods we have sent to relieve the famine, remarkably little has on the whole been stolen, whether this be due to the fact that Red soldiers have to a great extent guarded it, or to the population having pious feelings with regard to the relief work, or both together.

For the rest, I am convinced that the sharpest measures to secure control and the most iron severity in suppressing the misdemeanours will not have so much effect as the raising of the railway workers' wages would have.

I hope that this study of the real state of the Russian transport system, made in quite an objective spirit, will be of some use to those who desire without preconceived opinions to become acquainted with the economic conditions of present-day Russia. To those who speak of the "catastrophic condition" of the Russian railways I would answer that, whereas the number of available locomotives in 1919 and 1920 had gone down to nearly 4,000, the number of locomotives in use in September, 1922, was at least 6,700, while the number of goods wagons in use was over 260,000.

If, however, one is inclined to infer from this that all goes well in the land of the Soviet, it is well to be reminded that these figures were respectively at least 17,000 and 500,000 before the war.

The statistics quoted show at any rate that Russia is an economic factor in Europe which must be reckoned with, and that the restoration of trade with foreign countries is not rendered impossible by the condition of the railways.

CHAPTER V

TRADE

If the best means of combating the economic disorder from which Europe is suffering is to facilitate and strengthen international relations ; if the neighbouring peoples must again become " communicating vessels " in order that normal life may be restored ; then the first question that arises with regard to Russia is this: " Can permanent relations with Russia be resumed? "

We have seen that Russian transport suffered greatly during the war and the revolution, and yet that it is capable of doing important work. In regard to this, therefore, there is no insuperable obstacle.

But with whom in Russia are we to establish relations? What organisation for purchase and sale is there, which can be used in establishing a regular system of exchange between foreign producers and Russian consumers, and between Russian producers and foreign consumers?

The answer to this question to-day differs entirely from what it would have been two years ago. At that date all commercial activity was illegal in Russia ; the whole apparatus of economic distribution had been nationalised, and was directly dependent on the State. But after the spring of 1921 the home trade or inland trade was again released, and little by little it has cast off to a considerable extent the shackles that cramped its development.

It is unnecessary to point out further that the Soviet Government's suppression of private trading was a grave error; that its attempt to organise economic life without money, and to distribute its products by means of State institutions, was an utter failure.

The majority of Bolshevik leaders admitted this, and sought to excuse these unsatisfactory measures by asserting that they were merely a further development of the same policy of State socialism to which the Tsarist and Kerenski Governments, as well as many other Governments, resorted during the war. The explanation, which is not without an element of truth, shows how greatly the ideas of the Soviet leaders have changed, for it is obvious that pure Communism in practice means the socialising both of wealth and its production.

In terms suited to the Soviet journals in which his article appeared in December, 1922, M. Lejava, President of the Home Trade Commission of the Council for Defence and Labour, has described the changes brought about by the new economic policy.

The disturbance of trade began as far back as the commencement of the imperialist war. The introduction of militarism in industry, the regulation of prices, the cessation of foreign trade, the increased issue of notes, the high prices, and speculation—all this began with the first days of the war, and gradually increased, until, at the end of the World War and the civil wars, our national economy lay in ruins.

The circulation of goods had been reduced to a minimum, communication between the different parts of the country had ceased, the consumers themselves were looking—often in vain—for the producers, there was a shortage of foodstuffs, prices were rising enormously.

The conclusion of the civil war liberated transport, harbours and telegraphs, for the ordinary work of peace-time; it has become possible to replace the requisition of agricultural produce by a tax in kind, and the peasant has been given the right to sell his surplus foodstuffs freely on the market.

The State institutions, Co-operative Societies, and other organisations which had stocks of nationalised goods at that time, the nationalised industrial enterprises, and private individuals, were given the right to realise their products on the market.

This was the beginning of the new economic policy; in fact it *was* that policy already in practice.

M. Lejava has recently given me interesting particulars regarding the progress of home trade in Russia and the difficulties it has to face. He observes that the goods which came on the market when trade was resumed were partly foodstuffs produced by the usual labour of the peasants, and partly textiles from the existing stocks. It was not until the latter months of 1922, he says, that the products of the organised industries, especially light industries, appeared on the market.

All this shows that the N.E.P. (everybody in Russia knows this abbreviation of the "New Economic Policy") was not due to a change of view on the part of any members of the Soviet Government, but was made inevitable by the force of circumstances. The State machine they had tried to construct would not work; during the winter 1920-1921 the inhabitants of the Russian towns were threatened with extinction from hunger and misery. The peasants, exasperated by the system of requisition, hid their produce. The State reserves were exhausted, and in spite of the most thorough search it proved impossible to find all the stocks in private hands.

N.E.P. was a better means than armed force to induce the peasants to put their produce on the market, and at the same time to bring the hidden stocks to the surface again. Private trading was once more recognised by law.

It was on March 21, 1921, that requisitioning was replaced by a tax in kind which varied according to the size of the farms and the harvest, but which had no legal right to go much over 10 per cent. of the latter. The peasants were allowed to sell the surplus of their produce in exchange for other goods in the local market, or through the Co-operatives. It seems, however, that this tax in kind has in some cases borne more heavily upon the peasants than the requisitions did, inasmuch as the tax (prodnalog) in 1922 realised about 5 million tons of corn, while the requisitions in 1920 only brought in 3·6 million tons.

The good effects of the changed system of collection have also been partly counteracted in some districts by the irregular taxes which have been imposed by all kinds of local institutions. Thus it appears from a recent official report that during 1922, in the Altai Government, the district Soviets, local Soviets, "committees for mutual help," etc., etc., collected 155 *illegal taxes*.

The central Soviet Government has just taken measures to counteract this extra taxation, and has decided that the peasants shall only pay "one single tax," to be paid in kind or with goods according to local conditions. Kamenev, in particular, spoke very strongly, on the occasion of the last congress of the Communist Party (April, 1923), against the imposition of illegal taxes upon the peasants.

The decrees of May 17 and July 17 (1921) permitted the handicrafts industry and the producing Co-operatives to realise their stocks in order to procure raw materials or such articles as they required. Barter, not trade by the medium of money, was supposed to regulate the relations between these small producers in town and country.

It was simultaneously decreed that the products of the larger industries should form a "State fund of Goods," the sale of which, in exchange for agricultural produce, was placed in the hands of the Co-operative Societies, and only in special cases of those of private commission agents.

It was soon discovered that the system of barter made business extremely difficult, and at the end of July (1921) the right was conceded to every citizen to trade in agricultural and industrial products, and also to hire the nationalised shops and stores which the Co-operatives did not claim. All trading, save in the goods which were a State monopoly, was permitted, and all traders had to be registered and to pay for a licence to trade.

It is important to note the prominent part that the Co-operative Societies play in this development. Nationalised in 1919, and transformed into a mere State instrument of distribution, they recovered in 1921 the character of private economic organisations. They continued, however, to be in close connection with the Soviet Government, which has its own representatives on the Co-operative boards of management. On the other hand, Centrosojus (the Central Union of Consumers' Societies) has to gather together for the State's account all the agricultural produce and raw materials the State requires. Goods from the State stores are given them in exchange. The exchange of goods by the official institutions, especially the industrial trusts, must go through Centrosojus, and they must not apply to other organisations except in cases where Centrosojus does not want the business.

I had a very interesting conversation with M. Khintchuk, the president of Centrosojus.

Our organisation [he said] consists of a union of 98 Government Co-operatives, embracing 700 District Co-operatives. These latter include 24,000 local societies, which control 40,000 stores.

Centrosojus lives on its own capital, and does not receive any advance from the State; whereas the Co-operatives in 1914 had sales to a value of 10 million gold roubles, the sales in 1922 rose to 66 million gold roubles in the case of Centrosojus and the organisations immediately dependent on it, and to 300 million in the case of all the branches.

The entire turnover of imports and exports by the Co-operatives from March 1922 to January 1923 represented a total of £2,000,000, of which three-quarters were exports, and one-quarter imports.

The Co-operatives have their own bank, the Svekobank, which is closely related to the State Bank. Khintchuk's right-hand man is at the same time the right-hand man of the director of the State Bank.

These two banks give the Co-operatives credit for the goods that are exported or ready for export.

Centrosojus has actually in its export stores reserve goods valued at 800,000 pounds sterling.

The connection between Centrosojus and the foreign Co-operatives is now quite normal, as it has been included in the International Co-operative Alliance.

M. Khintchuk expressly drew my attention to the fact that among the managers of the Co-operatives were not only Communists, but also people "without party."

The former president of Centrosojus is one of the chairmen of the new Co-operative Bank, as is also M. Arsarkhissov, the former president of the People's Bank in Moscow. M. Khintchuk has been in Centrosojus since 1906, and M. Schvetsov, his right-hand man, since 1910.

Centrosojus plays a part of immense importance in Russia, but its petty commercial methods and its bureaucratic organisation have been sometimes subjected to criticism.

I believe that the Co-operatives are, perhaps, one of the healthiest elements in Russia's economic organisation ; but membership of them, which was made compulsory at the time of nationalisation, certainly ought once more to be left to personal choice. The enterprise of the local Co-operatives is greatly paralysed by the deadweight of indifferent numbers who have to belong. I feel sure that it would be all to the good if the Co-operatives recovered their former character of voluntary societies.

An objection made against Co-operation, no doubt on good grounds, is that it can easily show good results in times when prices are rising, as it is in a position to sell its goods cheaper than the private merchant who is obliged to think of what it will cost him to buy in fresh stocks. But as it has been necessary in Russia to discard the paper rouble in account-keeping, and to take either the "gold rouble" or the "goods rouble" as a basis, the present period of falling prices is very unfavourable to the Co-operative Societies, and their financial position must now be a difficult one.

The Co-operative Movement has really found a peculiarly favourable soil in Russia. The old peasant institution of the *mir* (village) makes it easy to grasp the Co-operative principle, and thus it happened that even before Communism the really great value of partnership in work was very widely recognised in Russia. One may, perhaps, even say that a certain fear of individual responsibility, which is a characteristic Slav trait, has facilitated the evolution of the Russian Co-operatives.

As it was impossible for the Co-operatives to manage all that the Government wanted them to undertake, many State organisations arranged for the sale of their goods themselves. Many trusts, for instance, sell their goods through commercial syndicates, or establish their own stores, and try to realise their products on the open market.

As private trade has gradually developed, on the other hand, it has frequently happened that representatives of the private stores have offered the State trusts higher prices than the Co-operatives have offered, and that the trusts have preferred to sell their goods to the private stores.

According to a report received from M. Bogdanov, president of the Supreme Council of National Economy, the number of middlemen in the retail trade constantly increases. In July, 1922, some 38 per cent. of the goods was sold through private traders, while the Co-operatives did not sell more than 8 per cent. of goods.

In February, 1923, the president of the textile syndicate declared that in the course of eleven months 454,000,000 arschins (1 arschin = 28 inches) of material were delivered to the organisation of which he was the head, but that only 380,000,000 arschins were sold. While private trading, carried on in Moscow by more than 10,000 traders, had developed in a very favourable way, the syndicate had not succeeded in selling more than 34,000,000 arschins through its branches in that city.

That trade is still badly organised in Russia is a fact that even the Soviet press recognises. Manufactured goods have long been sold under the cost of production, and this has considerably reduced the working capital of the trusts. Since the beginning of December, 1922, the prices have risen so rapidly that the balance between agricultural produce and manufactured goods has been totally upset. Between October 1, 1922, and January 1, 1923, wheat has not risen more than twice, whereas the price of metal goods has been trebled and that of cloth quadrupled. One arschin of cotton material cost about 5·5 lb. of rye flour before the war. On January 1, 1922, it was not worth more than 3·8 lb. of flour, for the famine had caused a considerable advance in the prices of food. After October, 1922, the relative figures before the war were not only reached but greatly exceeded. One arschin of cotton material was then worth 9·4 lb. of rye flour, on December 1st. 13·5 lb., and on January 1, 1923, from 17 lb. to 18 lb. Such a rise in the price of industrial products can only lead to an interruption of the relations between town and country, and to a crisis in distribution.

According to a Soviet economic journal, vast tracts of the country are suffering from a terrible shortage of industrial products, while at the same time they possess great values in the form of raw materials.

> When the representatives of our syndicates and trusts [it adds] arrived at the Kirgjiz steppes to buy the flax which is so indispensable for our factories, and offered two arschins (56 inches) of calico for one pud (36 lb.) of flax, one can no longer talk of a trade crisis but of a tragedy.

When I was in Moscow in January and February of the present year I often heard from other sources about the acute crisis in the local trade. A noticeable increase in the rents of stores and shops, imposed by the Moscow Soviet, resulted in the closing of many businesses.

I have not disguised the very great difficulties that Russian trade has to overcome. But it must not be forgotten that the advance made in less than two years is enormous. Trade had ceased to exist, and now it has developed in three forms: State trade, Co-operative trade, and private trade. Life itself, competition, the serious efforts to secure a better technical organisation, will lead, I think, to a kind of *modus vivendi* being established between these three forms.

Whereas foreign trade was an absolute State monopoly in 1921, a number of Russian trade organisations have now received the right to trade abroad. It is true that the number of State institutions with this right has recently been reduced again, but several foreign companies have simultaneously been given the right to import and export certain goods. The Commissariat for Foreign Trade (Vnesjtorg) gets a good deal of the profit, but that does not prevent the private companies from organising their foreign trade in quite a practical way, at any rate to some extent. The State chiefly exercises control and takes part of the profits.

No doubt it is true that if private trading,—e.g., in corn—with foreign countries was released, the prices on the home market would rise considerably. The State Bank could then no longer buy corn at a price of six to eight dollars a ton and sell it again in Finland at forty-two dollars, thus increasing its stock of gold to cover the issue of tchervonets in sufficient numbers (Cf. the next chapter). But the reduced purchasing power of the country population which results from these restrictions is so fatal for Russian industry, and causes such wide disturbance in the economic life of the country, that they cannot continue in force longer than is absolutely necessary.

The Vnesjtorg seems thus to be gradually developing into an instrument of control instead of a clumsy State apparatus for direct trading.

It cannot, however, be denied that even the control exercised by the Vnesjtorg over foreign trade is liable to destroy confidence in Russian commerce. Thus in Norway, for instance, we have cases such as that which occurred as recently as in May of this year, when the director of a branch of the Economic Council in Russia opened negotiations, from a large Russian port, with a Norwegian firm concerning the sale of Russian wood in exchange for Norwegian fish ("fat-herring"). In response to an explicit inquiry the director gave an assurance that the necessary licence for this transaction was guaranteed by the Russian authorities. The contract was duly signed, and the Norwegian firm made all its arrangements and re-sold the Russian goods; after which it received an intimation that the Vnesjtorg had refused to grant a licence for the transaction which had been effected, because the price of the herring was considered too high. This latter assertion is apparently due to the failure of the Russian authorities to realise that there is a considerable difference between the price of fat-herring and that of spring-herring or of large-herring.

The Norwegian firm lost money on the business,

and it is obvious that such occurrences in the case of transactions arranged with Russian official institutions are bound to weaken the belief in really sound business relations with Russia. The cause of the mistake in this instance is difficult to trace ; but presumably it is due in the main to a lack of co-operation between the various Russian organisations, and to the excessive bureaucratic tendencies which seem at present to form a serious obstacle in the way of the development of Russian economic life. An experience such as that mentioned above is a warning to foreign business men to secure the written consent of the Vnesjtorg first of all, where imports to, or exports from, Russia are concerned.

In other cases it has similarly proved to be a matter of great difficulty to obtain sufficiently reliable agreements with the Russian State authorities. Probably this is owing both to the frequently clumsy working of bureaucracy and to the already mentioned lack of co-operation between the Russian State organisations ; and let us hope that this will soon right itself as a result of more experience. But in the meantime it has had a very unfortunate effect on outside confidence in Russian trade possibilities.

What is first and most urgently needed for the recovery of Russia's home and foreign trade is capital. The various undertakings lack the necessary working capital for procuring raw materials in time and for giving short-term credit to the Russian population, whose purchasing power is greatly reduced.

I have not spoken of the well-known "mixed companies," which the Russian Government has suggested forming together with foreign capitalists who want to work in Russia. These companies were to consist only partially of foreign capital, while the Russian Government was also to have a part interest in them.

Such an arrangement might have some advantage and some drawbacks which are fairly obvious. It is clear that this would render the Russian authorities more interested in the working of the companies, and would help to secure facilities.

But, on the other hand, the advisability of the State interfering with the actual working of the companies is doubtful. One of the great German industrials who has tried to secure a concession for large undertakings in Russia told me that he might, perhaps, go so far as to let the State have the economic direction of the undertakings, though that was rather a doubtful step to take ; but he would have to reserve wholly to himself and his shareholders the technical direction, for this absolutely depended on expert knowledge.

I think that these mixed companies have the most chance to succeed when they are organising the export of raw materials, the exploitation of which is not too complicated (e.g., timber and petroleum).

Seeing that no considerable participation of foreign capital in private Russian trade is likely as yet, it appears to me that healthy and lasting connections may most easily be established by dealing with the Co-operative Societies.

One objection frequently heard outside Russia is that regular commercial relations with that country cannot be developed as long as personal security is so inadequately safeguarded by law within her territories.

It cannot, I think, be denied, that all the machinery of political activity, with its secret police —the tcheka, or G.U.P., as it is now called— has greatly undermined confidence in Russian conditions generally. Many people, including foreigners, have suddenly and unexpectedly been arrested and kept in confinement for a long time, without any proper legal inquiry and without any satisfactory explanation of the cause of their arrest. In the case of foreigners, " commercial espionage " has frequently been given as the reason.

Very naturally this procedure has made an extremely unfortunate impression outside Russia, where personal liberty and legal security are recognized as being the greatest and most inalienable benefits.

On the other hand, it should be remembered that the legal right of personal security has never been strongly safeguarded in Russia. Even in former times numbers of people were suddenly and unexpectedly imprisoned merely on the charge of so-called dangerous political opinions, or even on account of so-called unorthodox religious views. They were often ruthlessly incarcerated in the fortress of Peter Paul, or were sent, without trial or sentence, to Siberia.

This ancient system appears, however, to have

been largely developed since the revolution. There can be no doubt of its unfortunate influence upon the evolution of stable conditions.

But such phases come and go in the history of nations. Let us hope that life itself will ultimately claim its rights in this, as in other directions, and will bring about a more settled and legally regulated state of affairs, much to the advantage of the whole community in its progress towards sound health.

CHAPTER VI

RUSSIA'S FINANCE

As we have noticed in Chapter III, the Soviet Government tried to get the "money" factor gradually eliminated from Russia's economic life.

In a communist State this medium of exchange is really unnecessary: the nationalised products of industry and the peasants' produce, after subtracting what is needed for their own use, passes into a State fund, and the State distributes it among the consumers. Any surplus of goods is disposed of on the foreign market through the publicly authorised channels.

Bank credit is also unnecessary: the Government, controlling products of all kinds, supplies the various economic organs of the nation with whatever they require. The peasant hands over to the State his corn, flax, milk, cattle; but has a right to receive in return from the State all the manufactured articles he needs; implements, clothing, footwear, agricultural machinery, etc. The workman receives a "pajok" (food ration), and cards authorising him to procure whatever he needs from the State's stores.

The State budget was to be calculated *in products*, and no longer in money values.

The Soviet Government, needing money to carry on its foreign and civil wars, decided that a largely inflated note-issue was very good business; for while it supplied the financial medium of exchange that they needed at the moment, it simultaneously brought about a gradual decline in the value of the rouble, and so made it easy to introduce the communist system, in which money was no longer of any account.

This policy was only too successful in causing the value of the rouble to fall with headlong speed. But in the spring of 1921, when the new economic policy acknowledged the important part normally played by money in economic life, the problem of Russia's financial reconstruction and the stabilisation of the rouble appeared in all its terrible gravity.

The attempts made by means of decrees to check the decline in the value of money were a total fiasco. It was all very well for the Commissariat of Finance to lay it down in 1921 that the gold rouble (2·66 gold francs) was not worth more than 30,000 Soviet roubles: in December the State Bank's official quotation was 58,000, in March 1922, 260,000, and in April 500,000. To-day a gold rouble is worth 25 or 30 million paper roubles of 1921, according as one takes the official exchange or that of the Black Bourse.

I may add that the Finance Commissariat, by a remarkably simple regulation which has worked very well, has partially counteracted the difficulties naturally caused by the use of such "astronomical numbers" in accountancy; it decided that the rouble notes issued in 1922 were worth 10,000 roubles of 1921, and that the roubles of 1923 were worth a million.

The success of this makeshift, and the readiness with which it was received by the population, shows that the paper money which the Soviet Government issued in order to cover the deficit on its budget has no longer any normal money value, and that it could not be taken as a basis upon which to reconstruct the financial organisation of Russia.

A simple instance will show how all banking and trust operations are rendered difficult by the variability of the exchange. The first meeting of the shareholders of the Industrial Bank was held in October 1922. The first action they had to take was to calculate the loss sustained by the bureau of organisation owing to the shares having been originally paid in kind. According to the commission of control the bank had on deposit 9 billions (9,000 milliards) of Soviet roubles, equivalent at the day's exchange to more than a million gold roubles. The stock of goods was valued at 1·5 million gold roubles. As the capital of the bank, according to the number of shares issued, ought to have been 3,300,000 gold roubles, the loss inflicted on the bank by the depreciation of paper roubles even before it commenced operations was no less than 800,000 gold roubles. The shareholders who had paid in kind, had to cover the deficit by further deposits.

Let us endeavour to review the efforts that have been made to reorganise the Russian finances by the Finance Commissariat, the State Bank, and the various commissariats and economic organisations whose aim is to restore the national credit.

In October, 1917, at the beginning of the Bolshevik revolution, 18·9 milliards of paper roubles were in circulation, and their value was reduced to one third (1 pound sterling was equal to between 27 and 30 roubles on the London Exchange).

The volume of paper increased rapidly; in January, 1919, it had reached 60·8 milliards, in January, 1920, 223 milliards, and at the beginning of 1921, 1,168·6 milliards.

The introduction of the "new economic policy" again rendered money necessary for economic operations, and still further stimulated the issue of notes. By January, 1922, the volume of notes had risen to 17,539 milliards.

Concurrently with the increasing volume of notes the gold-value of the Soviet rouble sank between January and May with even greater rapidity. Even when notes were issued *every month* equal to more than half of the total amount of notes previously in circulation, the rouble's decline continually reduced the value of the total amount of notes, and in so doing reduced the State debt.

For instance, when the note-issue in March, 1922, was equal to over 32 billion roubles (a billion = one million millions), and raised the total amount of notes in circulation from 47 to 79 billions, the value of the whole circulating volume of paper, calculated in pre-war roubles, declined from 104 millions to 88 millions.

In the course of the summer months, on the other hand, the development of trade, as a result of the country's new resources furnished by the harvest, induced a partial stabilisation of the rouble. Though the speed of the issue of notes has noticeably fallen off since then (in November only 30 per cent. of the notes in circulation was issued), yet the gold-value of the total amount of notes (which had dropped in May to 57 million pre-war roubles) has gradually risen. At the end of August it had reached 137 millions, and at the end of October 185 millions of pre-war roubles.

It is important to notice that although the Soviet Government's note-issue is still enormous, it is not haphazard, and a real effort is being made to reduce its proportionate dimensions. In particular it is encouraging to convert the monthly issues during 1922 into pre-war roubles and compare them with the sum of the Russian Government's normal sources of income in kind: taxes and receipts from the State's property and enterprises. We are then able to see how these normal sources of income are gaining in importance. Whereas in January, 1922, they did not amount to more than one-eleventh of the note-issue, they advanced in April to more than one-fourth, in August to more than one-half, and in October to more than three-fourths of the amount of notes put in circulation. This may be seen from the subjoined table :

	Billions of 1921-Roubles or Millions of 1923-Roubles.		Millions of Pre-War Roubles.	
	Issues.	Taxes and Receipts.	Issues.	Taxes and Receipts.
January (1922) ..	12·6	1·2	40	3·7
April (1922) ..	46·6	13·4	16·4	4·7
August (1922) ..	221·3	122·2	41·9	23·2
October (1922) ..	304·1	235·9	37	29

The movement described above continued in November and December. In the course of the last three months of 1922 the total of taxes and receipts very nearly reached the figures for note-issues, which were 1,143 million roubles of 1923.

These results, which are still rather uncertain in some respects, have been obtained by imposing a series of direct and indirect taxes (industry tax, civil tax : on income and capital, stamp duty, excise, customs, etc.), and in addition innumerable local taxes.

Above all it should not be forgotten that, in spite of all these financial reforms, the Russian Government depends on the tax in kind, the well-known " Prodnalog," as its safest source of income. In corn or agricultural produce of various sorts the Russian peasant last year paid a tax to the State equal to 4·8 million tons of rye. This produce is used partly to feed and pay the State employees and the army, and partly for distribution in the famine districts as food for the people or as seed-corn.

It is a well-known fact that in June, 1922, the

Russian Government floated a corn-loan, i.e. it issued bonds, the face value of which was guaranteed by the tax in kind, collected in advance. The owner could send them back to the State when "prodnalog" was demanded, which was much more convenient for him than to transport corn, or else he had the right to draw during the winter the quantity of corn that his bond was worth.

At first the people received this loan enterprise with suspicion, but they soon discovered its advantage: the corn-loan bond furnished a "stabilised rouble."

Of bonds representing 10 million poods (= 160,000 tons) of rye, issued by the Finance Commissariat, 8 millions had been sold on September 1st, when the period of issue closed. The State Bank bought the remaining 2 millions and sold them again in September and October at a large profit.

The success of this first "corn-loan," which was an important step in the direction of substituting a money tax for the tax in kind, presents an interesting example of financial operations of quite a normal character carried out by the Soviet Government. It has certainly created a feeling of more confidence among the great mass of the peasantry, and opened the way for inland loans in future.

But the most important of the efforts made in Russia to secure a sound financial organisation is that made by the Soviet Government through the State Bank. At the Pan-Russian Finance Congress in October 1922, M. Sokolnikoff, Finance Commissary, introduced his plans as follows:

Our paper money is declining in value, because it has been issued in too large a quantity. At the same time the gold value of our whole note circulation is declining. Before the war there were 2½ milliards of gold roubles (Note: in coin and paper), in circulation, whereas the actual value of our whole note circulation now is not more than 150 millions. As the distribution of goods increases and trade and industry develop, the country will consequently need a larger amount of money than there is now in circulation.

It would not be wise, therefore, to discontinue the issue of notes altogether. In reality there are two kinds of issues: one which serves to cover the deficit on the budget, and another which aims at giving credit to production. The first is always harmful, but the second may be useful if it is employed in a sensible way.

Up to now these two issues have consisted of paper money put in circulation by the State Treasury. Henceforward these two categories will be separated; the treasury issues will be for State use and to cover its deficit, while the other kind of issue will consist of bank notes with a gold value, issued by the State Bank.

In November, 1922, the first series of 200,000 tchervonets (1 tchervonets = 10 gold roubles = 26·6 gold francs = £1·05) in bank-notes was put into circulation; it was part of the first issue fixed at 500,000 tchervonets. It was fully covered (100 per cent.), by gold or stable foreign bank-notes (dollars and pounds sterling), and not merely to the extent of 25 per cent. as proposed in the edict of October 11th.

The bank-notes were at first delivered only as an advance on the security of goods or bills, but after December 5th the bank sold bank-notes at the preceding day's rate of exchange on the Commercial Bourse in Moscow.

Thanks to the care with which the issues have

been managed, the bank-notes have very nearly retained their gold value. Thus on February 7, 1923, when the gold rouble was worth 21·50 roubles of 1923 at the official exchange, and 27 roubles on the Black Bourse, a tchervonets note was worth 220 roubles of 1923. On April 16th tchervonets stood at an exchange of 400 paper roubles (of 1923), or the same as pound sterling. In special circumstances, however, it would seem possible for the tchervonets to fall below its gold parity ; as now at the beginning of May, for instance, owing to the fears entertained regarding a possible break in the trade relations between Russia and Great Britain.

The unpleasant part of this arrangement must be said to be the circumstance that the State Bank obtains the gold needed to cover the tchervonets largely at the expense of the peasants : as stated in the previous chapter, it buys their corn at a price of six to eight dollars the ton, and sells it in Finland for forty-two dollars. The ridiculously low price on the home market is a consequence of the State monopoly, which prevents the peasant from selling his corn direct to the foreign purchaser.

I had a long talk with Mr. Scheinman, president of the State Bank, regarding the organisation and working of his bank. The office for bank-note issues is almost entirely independent, and its manager is a well-known Russian financier, M. Koutler, who was formerly Under-Secretary of Finance under the Tsar's regime. "He is a bureaucrat," said M. Scheinman, "who will never put his signature to the issue of new notes until he has received the regular gold cover for them."

On February 1, 1923, the balance sheet of the office for note issues was as follows:

Assets.	Tchervonets.
Russian gold coin	866,000
Gold bars	244,703·7
Foreign gold coin	28,073·7
Stable foreign banknotes (£ and $) at an exchange of 0·9 tchervonets to the £	384,412·5
Pound bills with 10 per cent. discount	245,158·6
Short-term securities and bonds in tchervonets with 10 per cent. discount	911,069
Total	2,679,417·5

Liabilities.	
Bank-notes sent to cashier's department	1,930,000
Balance available for issue	749,417·5
Total	2,679,417·5

The balance sheet of the Russian State Bank to date March 16th this year gives the position thus:

Assets.	Tchervonets.
Russian gold coin	866,000
Gold bars	1,020,727·4
Foreign gold coin	28,073·7
Stable foreign bank-notes (£ and $) at an exchange of 0·9 tchervonets to the £	457,912·5
Sterling bills	304,560
Bills in tchervonets discounted	830,308·1
Bonds in tchervonets with security in goods ..	1,139,646
Total	4,647,226·7

Liabilities.	
Bank-note issues	3,700,000
Balance available for issue	947,227
Total	4,647,227

It is unnecessary to emphasise the fact that the amount of tchervonets put in circulation, and which, according to the last quoted statement is equivalent to 37 million gold roubles, is exceedingly small compared to the country's requirements. I have entered rather fully into the question of bank-note issues, which go on side by side with the issue of Soviet roubles, because it proves that the Russian Government understands the necessity of creating a stable and healthy financial organisation. It is of greater importance in estimating the condition of Russia to-day, to mark the direction of its efforts, than to measure the results it has so far achieved.

Space does not permit me to mention all the details M. Scheinman gave me about the operations of the State Bank, which has more than 170 branches in all the important towns, and correspondents in many of the smaller ones. It undertakes all transfers in Russia and from abroad to Russia. If the senders do not express a wish to the contrary, it pays in foreign currency all transfers of dollars or sterling in order that the recipients may not incur loss through the decline in Soviet roubles.

(In the interval since the above information was issued, however, the state of affairs appears to have altered, judging from a report, dated April 30th, from my representative in Moscow. The State Bank was then unable to pay us a dollar check, but offered pound sterling instead, or the corresponding value in Soviet roubles at the exchange of the day (102 roubles to the dollar), or tchervonets at the day's exchange. Dollars could possibly be paid in three or four weeks' time ; but that was not certain. In response to a request to transfer money (dollars) to Odessa, the reply was received that it was absolutely *prohibited* to transfer foreign money from one part of Russia to another. When reference was made to what M. Scheinman had stated to me, namely that the bank could always undertake transfers and payments of foreign currencies, the answer received was that that conversation was at least a month old, that there had been changes in the Government's financial policy in the meantime, and that what the officials of the bank proposed to-day might very well be changed a little later.)

M. Scheinman further informed me that the State Bank shows great caution in furnishing industry and agriculture with credit. The amount of the credit and interest is fixed in tchervonets ; debtors have to repay the gold-value in tchervonets or Soviet roubles at the current rate of exchange.

The State Bank only finances undertakings which do not run at a loss, and leaves the State Treasury to provide capital, if it can, for undertakings which do not pay their way.

The Government is interested in the success of the bank-note issue for two reasons :

1. As it no longer has to finance undertakings which pay their way, it can reduce its note issue of Soviet roubles proportionately.

2. As part of what the public pays for State administration (railways, post, customs, etc.), is paid in tchervonets of stable value, the steady decline in roubles will not inflict such large losses on the Government.

M. Scheinman very kindly allowed me to see

over the various premises of the State Bank; especially the great armoured vaults, where the gold and stable foreign currencies covering the "tchervonets," and also the bank reserves, are stored in huge safes.

He also spoke of the development of the State Bank's business, which would ensue when the credit institutions in every country entered into regular and direct relations with it.

In the course of one year's working the State Bank has collected a considerable supply of bills, only including bonds in undertakings which do not *run at a loss*. One of its great tasks has been to finance Russian exports. But it has too little capital for this work, or for allowing its branches to launch out into great activity. Its rapid development would be very greatly facilitated if foreign countries would give it credit in the three following ways:

1. Advance on bills.
2. Credit on goods.
3. Credit to industrial trusts in Russia against the State Bank's guarantee.

In addition to the State Bank, the last few months have seen the formation of numerous industrial banks, trade banks, agricultural banks, and mutual credit societies. Some of these institutions are very important, but, of course, they are very far from being able to secure the credit which is indispensable for the country. This question will be discussed in the succeeding chapters on agriculture and industry.

CHAPTER VII

AGRICULTURE

IN the preceding chapters I have more than once alluded to the importance of Russian agriculture. I pointed out that the Soviet Government's decision, in the spring of 1921, to change its methods and launch the "new economic policy" was due, above all, to the bitter antagonism aroused among the peasants by the system of requisitions, and to the perilous reduction in the agricultural output which resulted.

I do not think that it is necessary to analyse all the factors which brought about the decay of Russian agriculture after the war broke out in 1914.

The mobilisation of 17,000,000 men and 2,000,000 horses during the first three years of the war, was in itself a very serious loss to agriculture; and their transport, together with all the provisions necessary to maintain them on the various fronts, monopolised the railways and waterways. This led immediately to a reduction of the area under cultivation; but in addition came the stoppage in imports of machinery and implements which were indispensable for successful farming.

It is true that the export of corn also ceased during this time ; but as the railways were unequal to managing the distribution of foodstuffs both to the armies and the civil population, the peasants were unable to sell their surplus produce, and this again led them to reduce the area under cultivation, although there was a serious food-shortage at the Front and in various parts of the Russian interior in the winter of 1916–1917, and a serious bread-crisis in January and February of the latter year in Petrograd and Moscow. Bread riots in Petrograd were the beginning of the first revolution in March, 1917.

But in addition to all this came the revolutions and the Bolshevik administration and the civil wars, and the richest provinces in Russia and Ukraine were trampled under foot and ravaged by the various armies in turn as they made their victorious advances.

We hear much, outside Russia, of the Red Army's requisitions and of the peasant risings that it suppressed. It is quite certain that the whole system of requisitions had an extremely unfortunate influence on agriculture, and this is even admitted by the Bolshevik Government ; but the system of plunder and terrorism initiated by the soldiery of Denikin, Koltchak, Petlura and Wrangel are only too readily forgotten.

But it is also true, as is mentioned in the next chapter, that the attempt to introduce the communist system into agriculture had a disturbing effect on the land conditions and temporarily checked the development in the direction of a better division of the land among the peasantry, which had made good progress during the years immediately before 1917, or rather, before the war.

Next, over and above all these calamities, came the terrible drought in the summer of 1921, which scorched up the Valley of the Volga, the lands to the east, and Southern Ukraine, and which dealt such a staggering blow to Russia's agriculture that it would unavoidably have caused an appalling catastrophe, if the Russian authorities and the foreign relief organisations had not partially averted the disaster.

It should not be forgotten that the Soviet Government actually sent nearly 600,000 tons of seed-corn to the famine districts in the autumn of 1921 and the spring of 1922. Thanks to the energetic measures that were taken, Russian agriculture, though still gravely crippled, is recovering little by little, and I am convinced that if it receives really adequate help it will sooner or later become even more highly developed than it was before the Great War.

As I stated in my first chapter, Russia produced between 1909 and 1913, on an average, more than a quarter of the annual cereal harvest of the entire world. She exported on an average 8·7 million tons of corn a year (the four cereals, wheat, rye, oats and barley), which is more than the total amount exported by Canada, U.S.A. and the Argentine together, on which Europe now depends for practically all its imports of corn. In 1913 Russia's exports of corn even exceeded 10 million tons.

At the same time Russia supplied Europe with nearly 8 million tons of forest products, 6,276,000 head of animals (she had more than 25 million goats, 37 million cows, 45 million sheep, and so on), and its dairy industry had made remarkable progress in the course of only a few years. The export of butter from Western Siberia, which was 2,600 tons in 1898, rose in 1906 to 48,700 tons, in 1909 to 58,000 tons, and in 1913 to 82,000 tons. In the months of June and July ten to fourteen trains, each with twenty-five wagons of butter, left Siberia every week.

Between 1907 and 1911 between 300,000 and 350,000 tons of hemp, and especially of flax, were despatched abroad annually.

On the other hand, Russia's and Siberia's 100 million peasants provided a vast market for foreign industry and trade, even if their annual purchasing-power was not put higher than 22 gold roubles and 43 kopeks (less than 60 gold francs or about £2 7s. 7d.), and it was gradually going up.

An interesting League of Nations report on the "Economic Conditions of Russia" describes in striking fashion the terrible decline of Russian agriculture during the Great War and the civil wars, and to this report I would refer the reader. This investigation is one of the few foreign economic publications concerning Russia which is inspired by a desire to understand the facts and to describe them objectively ; and it deserves notice that most of the statistics showing the decline in production during recent years were published, or officially sent to my representatives in Russia, by the Soviet authorities, who openly acknowledge the gravity of the situation.

I will only quote here two statistical tables, one which shows the reduction of the area sown and of the corn harvest, and another which gives the production of flax.

CORN IN RUSSIA (EXCLUDING THE CAUCASUS AND TURKESTAN).

Year.	Area sown (in millions of hectares—1 hectare = 2½ acres).	Crops (in millions of tons).
1916	90·8	65·9
1920	62·5	28·9
1921	54·0	26·9
1922	49·5	33·6

The fact that the area sown has decreased between 1921 and 1922, in spite of the new economic policy, is due to the famine caused by the awful drought in 1921 in the Volga regions and Southern Ukraine.

I believe, however, that the noticeable improvement that the harvest of 1922 has made in the situation is even more striking than appears from the table. It is true that I do not share the view expressed by some Russian statisticians that last year's harvest reached 2·8 or even 3 milliards of poods of corn (= 46 to 49 million tons). Those figures are certainly too high, and the fact that the tax in kind has yielded more than anticipated only shows, perhaps, that the peasants have been too heavily taxed. But the reports furnished to me by the Soviet authorities themselves and by my delegates show that the position in 1921 was even more serious than it appears from the figures of the Central Statistical Bureau, quoted in the League of Nations Report. The harvest in Ukraine, for instance, was one-half of what the official statistics state, although their figures for the total harvest in 1921 do not go higher than 26·9 million tons. If the figures for 1921 should be still lower than the table indicates, it is not surprising that last year's harvest, even though it was not much over one-half of a normal harvest, has nevertheless effected a great improvement in the food situation in Russia.

The cultivation of flax has also decreased seriously. Before the war there were about 1½ million hectares (1 hectare = 2½ acres) under flax, and the annual crop was 416,000 tons, worth 160 million gold roubles. Part of the crop was used in the Russian textile industry, and the remainder formed a valuable article of export, ranking third in importance after corn and timber. When the Bolshevik revolution broke out the cultivation of flax had already gone down by one-half, and the decline continued between 1917 and 1921 as follows :

Year.	Area Sown (thousands of hectares).	Crop (in tons).
1917	854	181,800
1918	836	172,500
1919	604	83,000
1920	529	73,800
1921	about 400	90,000-98,000

Although the crop increased in 1921, the area sown with flax had decreased. The cause of this decrease was that the price of foodstuffs rose during this famine-period much more than did the price of manufactured goods. Whereas prior to the war a kilogramme of flax was worth 5 kilogrammes of rye, in 1920 a kilo of rye was worth 2 kilos of flax, and in 1921 it was worth 5½ kilos.

It was therefore not in the peasant's interest to cultivate textile plants. After the harvest of 1922 the price of textiles drew level again with that of foodstuffs and then passed considerably beyond it. Whereas on February 1, 1923, the price of foodstuffs was 34 million times higher than before the war, the price of textile goods was 40 millions higher.

In 1922 the area under flax already began to increase. According to a report sent to me by the Supreme Council of National Economy, the quantity of flax offered on the market exceeded by two or three times what the Russian textile industry could purchase, although it had increased its output of textile materials by 82 per cent. as compared with the previous year ; but it was short of capital. The Government has decided to augment the export of flax to 40,000 tons in 1923. In the first ten months of 1921 it was only 5,200 tons, and in the corresponding months of 1922 it was 29,200 tons.

These two examples show with sufficient clearness that although Russian agriculture is beginning to recover, it is still greatly crippled. In particular the conditions are very serious in the famine districts, where the insufficiency of food, the shortage of seed-corn, and above all, the terrible shortage of animals, prevent the peasants from cultivating their lands on the former scale.

The necessity of coming to the aid of the peasants in their task was impressed upon me by the peasant who has become one of the leaders of the Russian State, M. Kalinin, President of the Central Pan-Russian Executive Committee.

The peasants in the famine districts [he said] are making remarkable efforts to renew their live stock. The animals have always been procured from the east, and before the war this was done in waves, as it were, of purchase, having an extent of about 200 kilometres. The peasants journeyed that distance in order to buy the animals they required in governments which in turn obtained their own requirements further to the east. The large decrease in live stock due to the Great War, the civil wars, and the famine, has caused these " waves of purchase," to extend as far as 400 or 500 kilometres, which means a considerable loss of time and power, for transport is difficult in the extreme.

The purchase of animals carried on by the Government in order to help the peasants in the famine districts, has unfortunately not attained large dimensions; it has chiefly served as an example and encouragement to the peasants.

In spite of the great losses sustained by the population, and in spite of the shortage of animals, eight million hectares were nevertheless sown in the famine districts in the autumn of 1922, which is 25 per cent. more than in 1921.

The Russian Government has just devoted 30 million poods of corn (about 490,000 tons) to the fight against the famine. In addition 30 per cent. of the civil tax, corresponding to very nearly one million gold roubles, has been allotted for this national work. We count on being able to feed 1½ million people until the next harvest, and that represents an expenditure of 15 million gold roubles, if we add the expenses we pay for the foreign relief organisations.

On the other hand the Russian Government has authorised the formation of an agricultural committee, which is to have a working capital amounting to 20 million gold roubles. This committee, which has branches in twelve districts, aims chiefly at giving the peasants credit, and helping them in every possible way to improve their farming.

But the work that needs doing greatly exceeds these modest credits. In the famine districts 1,600,000 peasants have no live stock. It would be a great thing if they could be supplied with stock, or if the draught animals could be replaced by mechanical traction. The import of tractors would therefore be extremely desirable.

If the foreign relief organisations, which have given us such generous help in the fight against the famine, could complete their work by providing the peasants with the implements they so urgently stand in need of, this would make it possible for them to work and manage by themselves.

After having endeavoured to restore economic life in Russia by favouring industry, the Soviet Government has now reached a full understanding of the decisive importance of agriculture.

In 1921 the Russian peasant was granted the right to dispose of the fruits of his labour. But the war, revolution, and famine have weakened and impoverished him, and deprived him of the implements for his work, and of his live stock, to a large extent, as well. His producing power, and consequently his purchasing power also, have largely diminished.

Among the real difficulties in the way of the recovery of agriculture we may further note, on the one hand, the fact that the peasants had again last year to give away a disproportionately large part of their crops, which cuts down their purchasing-power. On the other hand, the peasant can only obtain preposterously low prices for his produce on the home market, which likewise reduces his purchasing-power seriously, and partially neutralises the advantages of the right conferred upon him to sell the surplus of what he produces.

These low prices are due to the State monopoly in foreign trade which prevents the peasant from selling his corn directly to the foreign buyer, from whom he could get a price many times higher, up to six times as much as he gets in Russia. What this, in reality, comes to is that the State not only imposes a heavy tax on the peasantry, but also derives a large income at their expense by buying their corn and selling it abroad at a much enhanced price.

Formerly, 1 pood (= 16·4 kilos) of good wheat flour had a value (75 gold kopeks) equivalent to about 6 arschins (4 yds. 2 ft.) of good cotton material, whereas the peasant can now only get 1 arschin for 1 pood of good wheat flour. That is to say, he gets for his labour only one-sixth of what he got before.

For a shirt he would need 4 arschins, which formerly cost him 52 kopeks, or rather over half a gold rouble ; now he has to pay 4 poods (66 kilos) of flour for it.

As the peasantry form 80 per cent. of the Russian people, it is easy to see that the peasants' poverty prevents the reconstruction of industry, which is unable to sell what it produces.

Moreover, agriculture has to cope with other serious difficulties. Owing to the reduced cultivation of land, weeds have got the upper hand, and home grown seed-corn is often largely affected by this admixture. The menace of insect pests, especially locusts, has also grown worse on account of the large areas of uncultivated land and of proper means to fight against them. The locusts caused great damage last year.

A dangerous enemy of the Russian farmer is the host of field rats—the so-called *susliks*. These threaten to do great damage in a number of districts this year, as, for instance, in the Tsaritsin Government. According to statistics, at least one-sixth of the total Russian harvest is destroyed by *susliks*. In 1919 about 3 million dessiatines (a dessiatine is 2·7 acres) of European Russia were ravaged by these pests. In 1922 4,222,283 dessiatines in the Southern Volga region alone were attacked by them, out of which no less than 1,664,347 dessiatines were in the Tsaritsin Government. In addition, 30,326 dessiatines were attacked by locusts. The "Narkomtsem"—Commissariat for Agriculture—has estimated the damage done by the *susliks* all over Russia last year at about 900 million gold roubles, and wherever they had ravaged, only a mere fraction of the crop was saved.

The campaign against these destructive creatures will be carried on, and the Russian Government has voted considerable sums for that purpose in 1923, but it is not sufficient, and even the most fruitful regions of the Southern Volga, which have hitherto been free from them, are now threatened.

The above will show that the Russian farmer has on all hands great difficulties and enemies of several kinds to fight against ; his life is not an easy one.

What is the significance of the measures taken by the Russian Government in order to restore agricultural prosperity? What stage do these measures mark in the social development of Russia? And lastly, in what way can foreign nations participate in this work of fostering the agriculture of Russia? These are questions with which I propose to deal in my next chapter.

It is well worth while to study closely the conditions under which European and Asiatic Russia's hundred million peasants exist. To bring fresh life to the vast Russian and Siberian steppes, to restore relations between the great peasant populations of the East and the over-industrialised nations of Central and West Europe, would obviously affect the international economic equilibrium in a manner needing no demonstration.

CHAPTER VIII

AGRICULTURAL RECONSTRUCTION

THE true strength of the Russian Government, the secret which has kept it in power, although the really communistic party is only a small minority in Russia, is in my opinion the fact that it has allowed the peasants to retain possession of the land, and especially to occupy the large estate-owners' lands.

It is true that, according to the Land Law, which has just been made public, the land is the property of the State, and the peasants have neither the right to sell it or to mortgage it. But the Russian peasant is no lawyer, and provided he is sure that he can keep his "isba" (farm-house) and his fields until his death, that his children will have the prior right to the family property, and that he can sell his harvest as he likes, after paying the tax in kind, he does not worry much about whether he has only the use of the land or really owns it. This holds good as long as he remains where he is. But it is difficult for him to move, as in such case he does not have any rights in, or compensation for, the land he leaves. Thus he becomes more or less tied to the spot, and to this extent his liberty before the war has been curtailed.

Moreover, the Land Law leaves the municipalities the right to choose between the system of periodical division of the land, which was formerly usual in the villages, and the lasting right of cultivation that I have just mentioned. My impression is that the latter will probably be chosen nearly everywhere.

In Siberia this system had also been introduced to a large extent even under the Tsar, and when travelling there in 1913 I became convinced of its valuable effects, especially where the peasants lived on the actual land they were farming, and not in the villages. Here also the peasant was, as a rule, denied the right to sell the land he farmed.

As regards European Russia, it was after 1907, on the initiative of Stolypin, and as a result of his agrarian laws, that vigorous measures were taken to divide up the common lands of the villages into separate farms, and in this way to abolish the old system by which this common land was periodically parcelled out into innumerable patches among the village peasants. This system had obviously been a paralysing one for all reasonable development of the peasants' primitive agriculture. What was wanted was to gather each peasant's innumerable scattered patches of ground into continuous areas, which he could have as his permanent property ; and also to get him to move out of his village and settle down on his own land. Gradually the peasants discovered the great advantages involved in this arrangement, and the movement went rapidly ahead, especially after 1910.

The Bolshevik revolution in 1917, and the order to introduce communism in agriculture and in the right of landownership, stopped the whole of this useful movement, at all events for a time. It is true that no real attempt was ever made to carry out these communist measures in the case of the peasants, who evinced a strong prejudice against them ; but a general confusion of ideas was brought about.

Meanwhile the peasants had driven out the landowners and had appropriated their lands. The land had also been taken away from some of the large peasant-owners. The smaller peasants were not inclined to give up this land again, either to a communist State or to the former owners. All through the last century the Russian peasants had fought to take the land away from these, who were looked upon as oppressors. At last their dream has come true, and even if it has not brought them the prosperity they expected, and even if they admit that they lived in better circumstances before, they can claim : the land is ours !

Communist principles will never become current among the Russian peasants. Despite the village system, with its common ownership, he is a thorough individualist, avoiding as far as he can all work for the common weal. And the experiments made in farming on communist lines by the Bolshevik administration were altogether a failure.

Opinion in favour of resuming the division of

the land is certainly growing stronger, and no doubt it will soon be carried on at an accelerated pace, even though it may have to be begun again practically from the beginning.

The Bolshevik leaders very soon recognised how hopeless was the endeavour to impose communism upon the Russian peasantry. Even in the spring of 1919 Lenin very wisely and very decidedly uttered a warning against it, and finally, at the communist assembly in March, 1921, he declared that the interests of the State rendered it imperative that its economic administration should be settled in accordance with the economic views of the peasant middle class, "which we have not succeeded in altering in the course of three years." In face of the peasants' opposition, the Soviet Government had to give in, as I have already said.

In general, the attitude of the peasantry towards the present administration is doubtless strongly influenced by the feeling that it has allowed them to take the land of the large estate-owners, which they had coveted so long. Otherwise they regard every government as a necessary evil, and they do not care much whether its colour is red or white, so long as it lets them alone and does not take the big estate lands away from them again. This explains why they were against Koltchak and Denikin, and, indeed, every general of the old regime; they were afraid of getting back their former overlords.

I am aware that the division of the land has reduced agricultural production by breaking up the large estates where the soil was more scientifically cultivated, and where the crop per hectare was considerably in excess of what it was on the land tilled by the peasants—relatively in the proportion of about 5 to 4, or even 4 to 3.

Nevertheless, I believe that this decline is only temporary, and that a considerable increase in aggregate production will come without restoring the large estates.

It should be remembered that Russian agriculture is so extensive and in general so utterly primitive that comparatively small improvements in methods and in implements will have a great effect on the total amount of the yield. As I mentioned in my first chapter, the pre-war production of the four chief cereals (wheat, rye, barley and oats) in Russia averaged 700 kilos per hectare (2½ acres) per annum, while in Canada it was 1,230 kilos. In Norway the average is over 1,700 kilos per annum. No doubt this difference is partly due to the dry Russian climate with the frequent droughts. But, nevertheless, it is certain that a little instruction and good example would achieve good results. The best proof that the Russian peasant is capable of improvement was seen in the enormous increase of butter production, brought about with the assistance of Danish dairy experts in West-Siberia in the course of only a few years, as was mentioned in my previous chapter.

One circumstance which should have an important bearing on this matter is the fact that so many hundreds of thousands of Russian peasants, now scattered all over Russia, spent several years as war-prisoners in Germany doing farm work, and learnt a great deal from German agricultural methods. In addition to this, many capable German farmers, who were taken prisoners during the war, have settled down as colonists, especially in Siberia.

As a preliminary to making any forecast concerning the development of agriculture in Russia, one must take account of the *human factor*, the psychology of the country population.

Like all peasants, the Russian peasant is a practical man. He has fought fiercely to conquer the soil, and the soil is his livelihood. He is ready to put as much work into it as will suffice to satisfy his wants.

But whereas the farmer elsewhere is an enterprising individual, comparatively well educated, and taking an important part in the public life of his country, the Russian peasant under the Empire remained in a state of ignorance and extreme misery. Weighed down by taxation, he had no hope of improving his position, and he passed his life in unrelieved poverty and often semi-starvation. The Russian agriculture which was so rich, taken as a whole, supplied him with few resources for his improvement; for the profits went chiefly into the pockets of the upper classes, and the middlemen who arranged about the exports. They contented themselves with squeezing the peasant, without ensuring him by any law the chance of improving his condition. In reality few really methodical efforts were made to replace his extremely primitive farm implements, such as the wooden plough, by modern implements and machinery. Living in his thatched hut, void of comfort and hygiene, he passed his days in primitive simplicity.

In order that the peasant, to whom the revolution has given the land, may farm it methodically and enterprisingly, he must be encouraged to improve his standard of life, and must at the same time be given the means of doing so. It will mean waging a fight against the tendency to revert to an even lower level than before, a tendency discernible in many Russian villages in consequence of the break in economic relations between the country and the towns brought about by the war and social disturbances.

A report on "Problems of Economy in the Country," which the Supreme Council of National Economy sent to me, states that since the revolution agriculture has not received value in manufactured goods equivalent to the farm produce supplied in the towns. "In consequence it cannot meet the reduced market in the towns and the loss of the foreign markets except by lowering its own production."

It is not enough, therefore, to supply the Russian peasant with machines and seed-corn. It is necessary to help him to rise to a higher standard of life, to improve his house, to build schools, to develop the ambition of the country population. At the same time the sale of agricultural produce at home and abroad must be reorganised; for it stands to reason that the peasant will not increase his production unless he can sell it conveniently and profitably.

Having reviewed this psychological aspect of the problem, let us see what has been and what ought to be done to solve it.

Recognising the impossibility of Russia's economic restoration until the great peasant population recovers its purchasing power, the Russian authorities have just appointed a committee, as M. Kalinin informs me, to furnish the peasants with credit. It is composed of representatives of the commissariats of agriculture, finance, industry and foreign trade, and of the State Bank, the Central Council of National Economy, the Co-operative Bank, and the central co-operative organisations themselves, etc. The chairman is the representative of the Pan-Russian Central Executive Committee.

Its object is to create a large number of small country banks, to which the State Bank and Commissariat of Agriculture will give a credit of 20 million gold roubles. The Co-operatives' bank and the State institutions and private individuals interested in agriculture will also participate financially in these banks. The peasant-co-operatives and peasants who put money into them will enjoy certain privileges; they will be allowed to postpone the payment of the tax in kind, and will receive interest at the rate of 3 per cent., calculated in gold value.

The credit given by these banks is limited to

a maximum of five years, and will help the peasant to buy agricultural machines, live stock, seed-corn, seeds and fodder. The deposits and loans will both be in paper money, but calculated in gold value. The Government will guarantee the operations of the new institutions.

Obviously the sum allotted by the Russian authorities is quite inadequate for the fulfilment of the Agricultural Committee's programme. No considerable help can be given unless this sum is greatly increased by the financial participation of co-operative societies *and private individuals*. Therefore the new organisation must succeed in inspiring confidence among the peasantry.

On the other hand, the enumeration of State institutions that are represented on the Agricultural Committee gives the impression that this young organisation may easily suffer from a certain bureaucratic character, that various influences may be brought to bear, and that it may be quite difficult for the executive to work energetically and unitedly for the reconstruction of agriculture. It is not without interest to remember that the financial commission appointed by the Supreme Council of National Economy came to the result, at the end of 1922, that even the agricultural credit which was given by the consumer-co-operatives' bank "did not reach the peasants themselves."

However this may be, the fact of the appointment of an Agricultural Committee seems to be a good omen. The Soviet Government tried at first to foster agriculture by creating and keeping up undertakings which were organised on communistic lines. Now it is understood that the only way to increase production is to give advances to the peasants themselves, to give them the possibility of making themselves economically independent. General prosperity is simply the sum of the prosperity of all the individuals.

It is further important to note that many institutions for granting agricultural credit are actually being formed in Russia, and that the peasants themselves are striving to improve their position. The peasant co-operatives, which have preserved the principle of voluntary membership, are very active organisations. Their object is to arrange the sale of agricultural produce, and on the other hand to procure for the peasantry whatever they require. At the end of 1922 some 25,000 societies were united in the "Pan-Russian Union of Agricultural Co-operatives" ("Selskosojus"), which includes 3 million peasant farms. These figures do not include the co-operatives in Ukraine, which have formed a separate organisation.

Selskosojus has just been granted the right to send its own representatives abroad; its operations will only be approved and checked by the Commissariat of Foreign Trade. It will aim at selling all kinds of agricultural products, especially textile raw materials, and will buy agricultural machinery and implements. Its work will increase manifold if foreign countries will show confidence and give it credit.

In spite of these signs of recovery, it must

be admitted that the position of agriculture as a whole in Russia is still very bad. Improvement is especially difficult in the famine districts, where the inhabitants have too often lost the courage and energy that are necessary.

Having sold everything last year to escape death, and being without the live stock indispensable for farming the land, the peasants have often sunk into a state of dangerous despair. If our help is confined to sending them food, they will get into the habit of being helped and will become idlers. What is wanted is to give them the means to work, to transform relief into work for economic reconstruction.

"The peasants ought to be assisted by advances rather than by gifts," declared M. Jakovenko, People's Commissary for Agriculture, in a recent conversation with me. "This is the only normal way, from an economic point of view, and it introduces a constructive element into the work of relief."

How can other countries assist in this reconstruction of Russian agriculture?

If important concessions of land were given to groups of capitalists, who financed and organised its rational cultivation, the general economic level might possibly be raised. But I believe that much quicker and more effective aid can be given in the form of helping the farmers themselves and their co-operatives.

It is vital that the Russian peasant should not get an impression that foreigners are exploiting the difficult position in which he is placed, and that they are coming to take the land away from him.

And, on the other hand, I do not anticipate any great results from foreign cultivation of Russian land so long as the country's general economic life remains unsound, as it must while want is the prevailing condition in the most fertile tracts of Russia and Ukraine. When in time foreign opinion gains confidence in the Russian peasantry, and gives credits to its representatives for purchases of machinery, seed-corn and insect-killers, and when the Soviet Government can simplify the bureaucratic organisation which still separates Russian agriculture from foreign capital, a co-operation profitable to both sides will at length become possible.

Without foreign help the recovery of Russian agriculture will take a long time and involve enormous sacrifices. When I lately drew the attention of M. Kalinin, President of the Pan-Russian Central Executive Committee, to the destructive effect on foreign opinion produced by the export of Russian corn, he answered that the Russian Government desired nothing more than to keep the whole harvest of 1922 to supply the famine districts. He himself anticipated that the number of persons needing relief would rise to nearly 5 millions before the next harvest, and to feed them all is a task far beyond the power of the Russian authorities.

But [he declared] what we are exporting is a minimum, forced upon us by the absolute needs of agriculture.

We export especially fodder, a little bran, selected oats, first quality wheat, etc. Our agriculture must really procure gold *at all costs*.

Last year it bought insect-killers at a cost of three million gold roubles, which have enabled two million dessiatines (about 5,000,000 acres) of cultivated land to be saved. Russia also has to buy annually eighteen million gold roubles' worth of vegetable seeds, clover seed, etc. This seed renders possible a harvest far exceeding in nutritive value that represented by the corresponding value in corn. Even from the point of view of the famine it is entirely in our interest to export a limited quantity of corn, in order to import vegetable seeds. It is a question of bartering corn for products which are in the highest degree necessities. If our agriculture only had gold, it would like nothing better than still to restrain the export of corn this year.

From the point of view of the famine this explanation is only valid so long as the Soviet Government really cannot export gold without seriously damaging the economic life of the country. Personally I believe that Russia's financial position is in reality exceedingly difficult, if not critical. In my opinion, therefore, the barter in question ought not to stop philanthropic relief.

Looked at from the standpoint of Russia's economy, this shows plainly enough how much her agriculture needs foreign help. It shows, moreover, that if normal co-operation is restored the Russian peasant will not long remain a debtor to foreign capital, and that it will not take long to set going regular distribution with properly organised channels of exchange.

CHAPTER IX

INDUSTRY

WE have already seen that agricultural production is the real motive power of the economic life of Russia. In particular its exports of corn would profoundly influence Europe's economic equilibrium.

Nevertheless, the country's industry, and not its agriculture, has chiefly engaged the attention of the Soviet Government until lately, which is easily explained by the fact that the workers formed a majority of the Bolshevik party's votaries. Nationalised industry, under the administration of the Supreme Council for National Economy and its delegates, has provided the experimental field in which the communist theories have been carried out.

That it has emerged from these experiments impoverished and disorganised is common knowledge. But it must not be forgotten that the Great War and the civil war had already dealt it a severe blow. It is not surprising, therefore, that the coal output in the coal-field of Donetz sank between 1917 and 1920 from 25 million tons to 4·5 millions, when we recollect that this field changed hands more than eleven times in that period, being won and lost in turn by the Soviet and the anti-Soviet troops.

It is unnecessary to take up much space here with a picture of the decline of Russian industry between the end of 1917 and the beginning of 1921, when the "new economic policy" was adopted, with results which I shall endeavour to outline. A few figures will suffice to show how production went down at an uncanny pace until the spring of 1921, thereafter to rise again in a marked degree.

Year.	Output of Coal in millions of poods (1 pood = 16·4 kilos).	Output of Petroleum in millions of poods.	Textile Industry, Cotton Yarn (in poods).
1914	—	—	23,588,000
1917	1,824.4	523	—
1918	730.3	233	—
1919	511	269	—
1920	466	234	825,000
*1921	472	235	1,075,000
†1922	592	283	3,056,000

* From October 1, 1920, to October 1, 1921.
† From October 1, 1921, to October 1, 1922.

These few statistics are sufficient to show that although the whole industry of Russia is beginning to rise from the depth to which it had sunk, its different branches are by no means equally situated. The lighter industry, manufacturing goods which find a ready sale on the market, is recovering much more rapidly than the heavy industry; the recovery of the latter within a reasonable time is, in my opinion, impossible without the aid of foreign capital.

As mentioned in Chapter III, the principle embodied in the "new economic policy," adopted in the spring of 1921, was the organisation of industry on a commercial basis. The smaller industries were handed over to private traders, while industries of medium size remained partially nationalised and were leased in part to co-operative societies and private individuals. The State retained control of the large industries, which were grouped in *trusts*, including a certain number of similar undertakings, textile factories for instance, or forming a combine of different branches of industry complementary to each other (e.g., coal, chemical products and glass). These trusts are subordinated to the Council for National Economy, which, however, has learnt by repeated experience the necessity of conferring on the management the widest possible financial and administrative powers.

The new economic policy has at once stimulated the production of articles which are in demand among the peasants, especially since the harvest of 1922, which to some extent gave them the means of purchasing. I have noticed the increased production of *cotton-yarn* between October, 1921 and October, 1922; this continued during the last three months of the year, when, according to a report just sent me by the Council of National Economy, the spinneries manufactured 1,053,000 poods, as against 333,000 poods in the corresponding period of 1921.

The improvement is still more noticeable in the manufacture of common *textile materials*: it has risen from 130 million arschins (1 arschin = 28 inches) in 1920–21,[1] to 446 millions in 1921–22, this being an increase of 343 per cent.

The *rubber industry* increased in 1922 4½ times as compared with 1920, and attained to over one-third of the production before the war. Its output, valued at 6,176,000 gold roubles in 1920, was worth 13,043,000 gold roubles in 1920–21, and 29,745,000 gold roubles in 1921–22.

The figures for the *chemical industry* are 42,300, 53,000 and 93,000 tons in the corresponding periods.

The *electro-technical industry*, which produced to a value of 5,034,000 gold roubles in 1920, declined in 1920–21 to 4,816,000 gold roubles, but soon registered a rapid advance. In 1921–22 it manufactured articles (including 2 million filament lamps) to the value of 11,938,000 gold roubles, and its production for the last three months of 1922 shows that the upward curve continues (6,122,000 gold roubles as against 3,689,000 in the corresponding period of 1921).

Russian industry is passing at this moment through a crisis in distribution owing to the population's diminished purchasing power. At the commencement of the working year 1921–22 it was selling its goods considerably below the cost of production, because, on the one hand, the pro-

[1] The business year in Russia is reckoned from October 1st to September 30th.

duction costs were excessively high, and, on the other hand, the famine sent up the prices of the chief cereals to a very high level. This was alluded to in Chapter V, and textiles were mentioned as one example; but the phenomenon even occurred in the food industry. The cost of producing 1 kilo of sugar corresponded to an expenditure of 10 kilos of rye, although one could not sell it for more than 7 kilos on the market. Consequently the factories lost 3 kilos of rye for every kilo of sugar bartered or sold. The industry thus suffered no small loss, the working capital becoming reduced to the extent of about 50 per cent. It was natural, therefore, for the prices of these products to rise after the autumn of 1922; but the drawback is that the rise in prices of manufactured goods means a reduction in the purchasing power of the peasants. This is specially important on account of the position in which it places the machinery and agricultural implement industry.

In spite of the inadequacy of the credit at the disposal of the State (500,000 gold roubles instead of 8,500,000 presupposed in the Government's plan), the agricultural implement industry succeeded in carrying out, between October 1, 1921 and October 1, 1922, 58·8 per cent. of its programme. It delivered, for instance, 40,277 iron ploughs, nearly a million scythes, and 700,000 sickles, and its output attained a value of 5,568,000 gold roubles, as against 3,125,000 in 1921. This is nearly twice what it produced in 1920, although it does not yet amount to more than one-tenth of the pre-war manufacture.

In spite of the urgent need of agricultural implements and machines in the country in Russia, yet a large quantity of these commodities are actually still stored in the State warehouses for lack of purchasers. The peasants are too poor to buy, and the industrial trusts, which have hardly any working capital, are not financially capable of supplying these implements on credit. They have not the necessary money to pay their workmen and to procure the raw materials needed for carrying on the work of manufacture.

M. Lejava, President of the Commission for Home Trade, has drawn my attention to the fact that the difficulty experienced by the Russian farmers in replacing their implements has made them very economical. Whereas a peasant would formerly buy a scythe every year, or every other year, he now makes it last three or four years. But it is obvious that this does not solve the problem.

> Capital alone [declared M. Lejava] will enable the factories to resume production and to sell at a moderate profit. They ought, moreover, to be so well founded financially that they could allow buyers to pay for their goods by instalments over a shorter or longer period. The terrible reduction of the people's purchasing power constitutes the main reason for the difficulties which beset our industry.

On the other hand, it should be noted that the light industry is further dependent on the heavy industry, which is very precariously situated. I have given some figures of coal and petroleum production; the improvement between 1920 and 1922 is obvious, but the output is rather small still.

In the Donetz coal field the crisis arising year after year, when the harvest draws the workmen to the villages, did not have so much influence on the output last summer as in 1921, thanks to the productivity of the miners who remained at work. From June to September 1·07 million tons were produced by 8,738 workmen, whereas 11,280 workmen obtained 0·65 million tons during the same period in 1921. But this increased quantity could not be secured without neglecting the timbering of the galleries and repairs, the lack of which constitute a danger for the future. The improvement in production during the autumn and winter was also smaller than in the preceding year. For the last three months, October to December, the production amounted to 1·7 million tons, which is half a million less than in the corresponding months of 1921.

Probably the result of the business year 1922–23 will not be good. The amount produced in the three first months of 1923 was 2 million tons, or 70 per cent. of what was pronounced necessary. This deficiency in coal production places a serious obstacle in the way of industrial prosperity and transport. During the year 1921–22 Russia imported rather more than 630,000 tons of coal, at a cost of 6 million gold roubles. But the financial situation is not likely to permit a repetition of such expensive importation as long as it is not counterbalanced by exports.

That the production of coal, like so much else in Russian industry, cannot be made to pay, is a grave difficulty. The workmen have been badly paid right up to the present time, and still the working expenses were very high. In June, 1922, for instance, it cost 62,000 roubles of 1923 to win one pood (36 lb.) of coal, while the management had to deliver the coal to the commissariat of transport for 28,000 roubles a pood.

A commission was sent to Donetz in September last to study the cost of production of fuel. It came to the conclusion that this was on an average 16·9 kopeks in gold per pood, but that it reached 39·61 kopeks in August at the time when the output was lowest. The amortisation of plant amounted on an average to a third of the production price, which proves that a proportionate reduction of the working expenses will not be possible unless the output is considerably increased. But for that, capital is necessary.

But it is the *metal industry* that causes the Supreme Council of National Economy most anxiety. The production of cast iron, for instance, was in 1921 to 1922 only 3·9 per cent. of what it was before the war, and the production of steel in Martin smelting furnaces was only 7 per cent. It is true that the situation is improving slightly. During the last three months of 1922, for instance, the production of cast iron increased 37 per cent. on what it was in the corresponding period of

1921, being 57,200 tons instead of 41,000 tons. The advance is still more noticeable in the case of the Martin smelting furnaces, which produced 107,000 tons of steel as against 70,400 tons.

These few figures only give a very incomplete idea of the condition of Russian industry. They are, however, sufficient to show that the increase of production is rendered exceedingly difficult by the lack of capital, and on the other hand that the new economic policy has rendered possible a notable improvement.

Nevertheless, one cannot close one's eyes to the fact that all the restrictions and monopolies constitute a serious danger, threatening the very existence of Russian industry. Nor should it be forgotten that its development last year was attained largely at the expense of the working capital.

Fresh capital is a crying need in order to replace or repair the worn-out machinery, in order to buy in time the necessary raw materials; and to be able to give credit to Russia's buyers, impoverished by the war and the revolution, Russia's industry needs foreign help. I am aware that those who have invested money in Russia earlier do not feel great confidence in the present administration, and I also know that several foreign Governments claim payment of the money owed them by the Tsar's Government.

It is not for me to discuss these claims or to offer advice to the Russian Government. I will merely express the hope that both sides will earnestly endeavour to find a solution which will make it possible to resume work together. I am very much afraid that if this does not come about, Russia will require a long time to recover, whereas her prosperity will be vital for the restoration of sound economic relations in Europe and the world at large.

I must add that I have been struck by the energetic and serious efforts by which Russia is trying to reorganise her industry. The disorder and anarchy which prevailed at the beginning of the revolution have been left far behind; the real danger now is bureaucracy far more than lack of discipline. The "Soviet workers" have no longer the right to interfere in the management of the business, and it is interesting to note that the average output of the workmen has gradually increased.

In Donetz, for instance, a miner in 1920 produced only 39 per cent. of the quantity of coal he was able to get in 1913. This monthly percentage of production rose in 1921 to 56 per cent., and in 1922 to 97 per cent. of what it was in 1913; but this latter percentage was only obtained by partially sacrificing important repairs, as mentioned above.

In the *petroleum industry* the large reduction in the number of casual workers employed has brought about an increase in the workman's average monthly production, which was 1,087 poods (17·184 tons) in October, 1922, as compared to 1,050 poods (17·23 tons) in 1913.

In the *textile industry* the output per worker in 1920 sank to 20 per cent. of what it was before the war. The percentage rose in October, 1922, to 64 per cent.

The *metal industry* registers the lowest output, 32 per cent. of what it was in 1913. But here, too, an advance has taken place; the figure was only 21 per cent. in 1921, and 17 per cent. in 1920.

M. Bogdanov, President of the Supreme Council of National Economy, whose courageous and methodical work for the regeneration of his country is well known, told me about the efforts made by the Russian Government to set industry on its feet again.

Upon the regeneration of agriculture [he said] depends the restoration of our entire national economy. Last summer's harvest was better, and the effect of that has at once been reflected in our industry, which has increased its production by 23 per cent.

As soon as the agricultural conditions improve, the peasants will have capital sufficient to enable them to begin buying, and so to put fresh life into our industry. The effect of this harvest has especially been noticeable on the textile industry's market.

As to the heavy industry, it cannot recover unless considerable credit is available. Foreign capital is therefore indispensable—unless, of course, a series of good years with rich harvests make it possible for us to raise the necessary working capital in Russia.

We hope even this year to improve our petroleum industry very considerably. We have sunk many wells and have purchased machines to expand our operations. In Baku we expect to increase the production by 30 per cent.[1] This will allow us to export petroleum, the sale of which together with timber will furnish us with capital. The requisite efforts to increase the output of coal and metals cannot succeed until we have secured the capital which it is unavoidably necessary to put into these undertakings. We cannot count on obtaining any large amount by exporting coal; the cost of production is too high, and moreover Russia always imported coal before the war.

Our *metallurgical industry* has had to combat many difficulties, but one can already discern considerable improvement in some districts. The smelting-houses in Ural have recently doubled their production. This is certainly due in part to the circumstance that they use wood and not coal in their high furnaces. Further, the population in this district, where the famine has been raging, have come to get work in the smelting houses and have been content to receive minimal wages. The costs of production have thus been reduced, and as is well known the iron smelted with wood (i.e. charcoal) is of much higher quality.

The general increase in our production this year is due to the fact that little by little the working has become more rational and less expensive. Our workmen work better than they used to do. We are advancing slowly towards the rational organisation of all our industries. By beginning with the regeneration of agriculture, and going on to the industries which require the least capital put into them, we count on being able gradually to amass the capital without which the recovery of our heavy industry is impossible. Thus we shall methodically raise the country's whole economic level. It is very clear that the help of foreign capital would render it possible to hasten the process considerably.

[1] A report just received from the representative of the export department of the Russian Naphtha Syndicate states that storage for 18,000 tons of petroleum has been hired in Hamburg, and in Wilhelmshafen, near Hamburg, for 12,000 tons. The Naphtha Syndicate's export department has also made a contract in Brussels with the Belgian Caucasian Company for the use of its installations for an annual quantity of naphtha up to 34,000 tons.

CHAPTER X

EDUCATION

ALTHOUGH the great universities were important centres of culture before the revolution, it must be admitted that intellectual life under the Tsar's regime was extremely artificial, and could not be regarded as a normally developed sociological phenomenon.

While the masses were plunged in profound ignorance, the aristocracy and the wealthy bourgeoisie, in touch with foreign countries, assumed a borrowed culture, often very distinguished, but as a rule extremely superficial. Russia gave to the world great men of science and brilliant authors, but her unbending and suspicious autocracy did not allow the intellectual life of the nation to develop freely.

Only a small minority had access to the world of ideas, and even then they became objects of suspicion as soon as any independent spirit of investigation prompted them to criticise the social or religious organisation of the country.

The fierce longing for education and liberty which tortured the country, induced thousands of students to emigrate, in their thirst for learning ;

they went to study at foreign universities, where they often lived in circumstances of great material hardship and want.

While the universities looked through their fingers in indulgent tolerance of the laziness of the young nobles who honoured them by attending them, sons of the peasantry and workers could not as a rule afford to go to the universities, and had but little opportunity for education, even if they showed special intellectual aptitude.

In education, as in the sphere of economic organisation, the revolution denotes a complete reversal of the situation. Compulsory and free elementary education was proclaimed. The attempt was made to organise continuation and higher grade schools on the principle that they were open to all young people who were able to profit by them, but only to these: mental capacity and work alone were to be taken into account.

Under the administration of M. Lunatscharsky, People's Commissary for Public Instruction, a large number of elementary schools were set up, and in these it was often endeavoured to introduce the latest educational methods. They formed the first step in the educational ladder, being compulsory, in theory, for four years. One-sixth of the best pupils, chosen according to their deserts, were to continue in a higher grade for five years; here they entered upon more or less specialised studies, according as they entered the divisions for industry, agriculture, etc. After this they arrived at the university, where the teaching of languages and literature and philosophy was reduced as much as possible in favour of the applied sciences, and still more the political and social faculty, where, as we know, Marxism was the official teaching.

On the other hand, in order to render it immediately possible for the workers to obtain higher education, a "workers' faculty" (Rabfak) was created at each university, where young people between eighteen and thirty years of age might study. They were selected from the factories and workshops on account of their ability, and were provided for by the State. 25 per cent. of them were to be chosen by the Communist Party, while 75 per cent. were to be elected, so the rule ran, by various Government bodies without political prejudice.

This gigantic programme was, of course, doomed to failure. Many elementary schools were opened, but for lack of means the majority of them were incapable of doing useful work. The teachers were very irregularly paid, and with long delays which inflicted upon them considerable losses due to the rapid fall of the rouble exchange. Thus they were reduced to poverty. And when, in addition, they did not receive the public ration (pajok), they often starved. Moreover, there was a great scarcity of educational material. What can the most self-sacrificing teacher do when his pupils have neither got pencils, copy-books, or slates and slate-pencils, and books are few and far between? Moreover, the war, civil strife, and not least, the famine in 1921, left entirely to the care of the State millions of orphan or abandoned children: 1,500,000 in the famine-ravaged districts alone. Inadequately as these little creatures were fed and clothed in the Soviet asylums, this still constituted a huge expense for the central and local authorities. It is true, however, that the foreign relief actions, especially the great American organisation (ARA) under the direction of Mr. Hoover, gave valuable help in this direction.

The truth is that the number of elementary schools has decreased so greatly that there are even fewer than under the Tsar's regime. I have received desperate letters from Russian teachers, whose schools had been closed for lack of funds. I have helped in a few special cases, and my relief organisation is, as a matter of fact, trying to send to Russia a little of the sorely needed school material, but it is necessary to devote a considerable amount of money to this work, which has such an important bearing on the future of Russia.

As a step in the direction of financial decentralisation, parallel with the general tendency of the new economic policy, the organisation and working of the schools have now been placed under the local authorities. It was the only way to save some of them; but it does not prevent the closing of many.

The Russian universities are also in great difficulties. The students were originally given their lodging and subsistence by the State, but now they have to keep themselves, except the poorest and especially those who are communists. In January, 1923, hardly one-third of the 120,000 students estimated to be found in Russia were receiving government rations, which are utterly insufficient. Moreover, quite high entrance fees have recently been reintroduced.

The international organisation for European Student Relief, which works with my organisation in Russia, has given valuable help to the Russian students: its representatives at the various universities have opened dining-rooms with daily meals for 30,000 students. It also does its best to supply them with scientific books. When one has seen these homes at the time when the students flock in for meals, and observed the happy expression on the faces of thousands of promising young men and women, one cannot but feel that a more satisfactory and important form of relief would be hard to find.

The fact that a large organisation of foreign students, whose political and religious ideas are to a large extent entirely opposed to the Soviet theories, has evinced such generous understanding of the great duties of international solidarity, inspires one with hope that the coming generation will be characterised by tolerance and a desire for peaceable work.

As for the Russian professors, their salaries are beggarly, and they are without the most necessary literary and scientific aids to study: books, foreign publications, laboratory apparatus and instruments, etc. Their position was particularly critical right up to 1922. I have heard of several cases of well-known professors who literally starved to death. Even at this moment the university teachers have many difficulties to contend with, and even if their means of subsistence may have improved they suffer greatly from their intellectual isolation. Such help as we have been able to give them, thanks in part to a certain number of foreign universities, has rendered it easier for some thousands of Russian professors to struggle through the worst period, but it is time that regular intellectual relations were restored between foreign and Russian universities.

By an order of December 28th last the Council of People's Commissaries exempted literary and scientific publications from censorship. Regular relations with the outer world were long rendered impossible by the atmosphere of political suspicion and organised informing which led to the imprisonment and often condemnation of many Russian intellectuals.

The Government's intolerance astounds and embitters foreigners, for whom liberty of thought and word represent an inalienable right. It is to be hoped that the Russian authorities will gradually understand this ; they should find it the easier, it seems to me, in that they no longer need fear any attacks from without ; and at home the political passions have cooled down. The reconstruction of the country's economy and resumption of methodical and peaceable work seem to be the general desire in all sections of the people, tired as they are of so many years' war and social upheaval. Leading professors who were not in any agreement with the communist theories, and who have suffered greatly during the revolution, said to me when I last visited Moscow:

"We are not Bolsheviks; from a theoretical point of view we are opponents of the present Government; yet we believe that Russia's economic position is so grave that all political questions ought to be relegated to a lower plane. We therefore co-operate loyally with the Government by continuing our university teaching, or by our common work in the various commissariats. We are convinced that in this we are doing our real duty and working for the recovery of our country's prosperity."

It is to be hoped that this loyal co-operation by non-communist elements will induce the Russian authorities to give up favouring, in the schools and universities, the professors and students who are communists. But Russia is still rather far from neutrality as regards tests of faith and politics in her educational establishments; though it should be remembered that the same was true under the Tsar. On the other hand it is only fair to recognise that the Bolshevik revolution, even in its most brutal periods, has shown comparative moderation towards genuine men of learning, compared to some other revolutions. They have been given, more or less regularly, official food-rations, and have also received much help from semi-official committees, such as Maxim Gorki's.

As a rule their books and laboratories have been respected, and as regards public libraries and museums, these have been considerably enriched by the nationalisation of private collections. Very little has been destroyed in this direction, and the first foreigners who were admitted to the Soviet museums were greatly surprised at the orderly and good arrangement of Russia's treasures of art and learning.

Why does the Soviet Government protect and even seek to develop public instruction?

To begin with, I think it was due to a serious desire to raise the intellectual level of the Russian people, and help it to rise above the condition of ignorance and superstition.

Next, and perhaps most, it was a means to convert the masses to the communist doctrines, I might almost say "religion." It must really be admitted that the Soviet Government has shown great ability in organising extremely telling propaganda throughout Russia's vast extent. By books, pamphlets, placards of all sorts, meetings and cinemas, it has sought to make "communist truth" permeate the Russian people, which until now has been less touched by modern intellectual movements than any other. The School naturally formed a particularly suitable medium for disseminating the official doctrine, and this is the reason why the Government would not allow any private educational establishments to be opened.

But now the Russian authorities recognise that the evolution of public instruction is closely dependent on the economic condition of the country. It is not enough for the Government to proclaim in theory that "the school and university are for all"; there must be funds to carry out this programme. After having undertaken the immense task of educating all the children in a nation of over a hundred million people, the Government understood that the financial means required were utterly disproportionate to the country's total resources.

On the other hand, higher education, of far too theoretical and political a character, has not achieved—from the point of view of communist propaganda—the expected results. The time for abstract discussions and revolutionary propaganda is past. The great work which has to be done now in Russia is the country's economic restoration—not the people's conversion to the doctrines of Marx and Bukharin. Many of the young people who have recently finished their university training stand bewildered in face of the technical problems which political discussions have not taught them to solve. They have difficulty in finding a place in the Russian organisations which are now being created on normal commercial lines, and they form a kind of new "intellectual proletariat."

Thus we now see an interesting tendency in Russia to put technical education first, as being more urgently necessary for the country than pure learning, and in particular than politico-social theories. The need is for practical men, and not for those who are looking for formulas and systems. And consequently the necessity is felt of increasing the much too small number of technical schools.

I have been told of several cases of young communists who took active part in the revolutionary movement and subsequently obtained quite important posts in the Government, and went to the university to finish their education. Usually they do not choose the faculties of philosophy or political economy, but the practical subjects such as mechanics, scientific agriculture, or applied chemistry. I have been told, for instance, of quite a young man who had long been a revolutionary, who became director of the service of compulsory work in Moscow, and afterwards of social work in Ukraine, and who has just entered the Moscow agricultural academy as a pupil.

The last Pan-Russian Soviet Congress expressed the wish that a certain number of students might be sent abroad to improve their scientific education. If a good reception is given to this " revolutionary youth," it will be a token that our scientific institutions are able to lay aside political divergences, and that could only strengthen the tendency in Russia towards placing technical ability before political opinions.

Genuine friends of the great Russian people can but wish that the generation which the Soviet schools are endeavouring to imbue with Marxian theories, may rather be attracted to practical knowledge. For when all is said and done, the only economic and social organisation of real value is that which is rooted in experience and everyday work.

CHAPTER XI

SANITARY AND SOCIAL PROBLEMS

THE health of the population of Russia was much lowered even before the famine in 1921, which in spite of the measures taken by the Government and foreign relief organisations, caused the death of at least three million people.

The Great War and the Russian civil war had in reality not only cost the lives of 3½ millions directly, but had in addition encouraged an unusual outcrop of pests: typhus, cholera, typhoid, intestinal inflammation and dysentery, which assumed an epidemic character and were spread far and wide by the movement of troops, refugees, and prisoners. Tuberculosis and digestive diseases had become widely diffused among the under-nourished population, living under the most unhygienic conditions, and the cases of premature ageing were innumerable.

The famine brought to light a whole series of illnesses, often caused by the use of harmful substitutes, and it led to a dangerous new outbreak of the epidemics. It is calculated that from 1918 to 1922 there were between twenty to thirty million cases of typhus. That means that during recent years the whole of Russia has been scourged with this epidemic, which has caused the death of vast numbers of persons, but has also made the population as a whole largely immune, as though by vaccination.

During these awful years the Russian medical institutions were disorganised in the extreme. Sanitary equipment and medical instruments have become more and more rare, and have been worn out, and the lack of medicine has become continually more urgent. The medical personnel has been in a situation of acute difficulty, especially in the famine areas. My delegates have reported several cases where doctors have died of starvation. And nevertheless, the Russian and foreign journalists who were on the spot during the most critical times reported the admirable courage with which the Russian doctors fought against the epidemics. Isolated in small towns where the death-rate was terrible, cut off from the centres of culture at home and abroad, they still did all in their power to improve the conditions by the use of such means as they had at hand.

Since the harvest of 1922 their position has naturally improved as far as food goes ; but the need of sanitary equipment and medicine is still very great. Decentralisation, introduced by the new economic policy, has deprived the medical institutions of the central authorities' grants ; they must henceforth depend on local contributions to pay their working expenses. It may easily be understood that such an arrangement, however admirable in normal times, plunges the sanitary organisations in the famine districts into terrible difficulties, since the local funds are very small and the strain particularly heavy. In co-operation with the Russian and Ukrainian Red Cross and the Commissariat of Public Health, my organisation has recently formed a committee for medicinal and sanitary relief, which sends to Russia completely equipped medicine chests, each sufficient for one thousand invalids for three months, and also a quantity of medical instruments. In this way a double object is secured: immediate aid is brought to quite a large number of sick people, and in addition the doctors, who were condemned to inactivity and despair through lack of equipment, are able to resume their activities, which are so essential for the improvement of their country's hygiene. It is thus an attempt to save the medical organisation and staff, whose destruction would be fatal for Russia.

Another social problem needing outside help for its solution is *unemployment*.

It may be said that the majority of the Russian peasants have always suffered under conditions of a sort of chronic unemployment. In the course of the long winter months only those who lived near the large towns could really count on employment, e.g., as cab-drivers. Only to a very small extent could the peasant home-industries ameliorate their position.

This long annual idleness of the Russian peasants is possibly one of the chief reasons why agriculture develops so slowly, and for the exceedingly primitive conditions under which the peasantry live. It would be a great thing to provide them with some winter occupation which would give them an extra source of income. Their home-industries might be encouraged and developed. In some districts, e.g. in Viatka and Vologda, they are of a very high quality. If their purchasing power increased, they could improve their farm equipment, and their wants would also develop, to the advantage of Russian and foreign industry.

I mentioned in the chapter on agriculture that more than $1\frac{1}{2}$ million peasants have lost their animals in the famine districts. M. Kalinin, President of the All-Russian Executive Committee, told me in February that there were also in the districts nearly 150,000 unemployed men (500,000 in all Russia). They were for the most part officials, officers or landowners of the old *bourgeoisie*, who found it difficult to fit into Russia's present social organisation. As they have never learnt any particular trade it is difficult to employ them in positions of great responsibility, M. Kalinin said, and still they must be given occupations which will permit them to live in a normal fashion.

The problem of unemployment is consequently quite different from what it is in Western Europe. The solution obviously lies in the reconstruction of agriculture, which will bring an improvement in economic conditions as a whole, whereas abroad the problem of unemployment can only be dealt with by a resumption of export.

M. Kalinin also mentioned the difficulty of the *war invalids*, for whom hardly anything could be done during the difficult years through which Russia has lately passed. Their number is comparatively fewer than in countries of the West, for owing to the hardships experienced in Russia a great number of invalids from the Great War have succumbed; while the civil war has created fewer of them, because its methods were at the same time less elaborate and more severe. According to Kalinin, however, there should be 200,000 to 300,000 registered invalids in all Russia, 65,000 of whom are in the famine districts.

> Help for the invalids [he said] is a question on which we lay special weight. It has been separated from the famine question, but the absolute necessity of finding a solution for it is now very patent. Considering their services to the country, and the bitterness they feel about being neglected, the invalids deserve to be treated with special generosity.

Here, then, the foreign philanthropic organisations can still find a field of usefulness and one whose unpolitical character is beyond dispute. It would be a great help to send artificial limbs, especially for invalids who till the soil.

A final problem of enormous moment for the future of Russia is *child-relief*.

In the campaign against the famine special relief was given to the children and some organisations have even allotted almost solely to children the foodstuffs they distributed in the famine districts.

This work has saved many of them, but the insufficiency of the relief given to their parents has created a fearful number of orphans. The number exceeds 1,500,000 in the famine regions, if we include children deserted or lost by their parents during the famine.

I believe that the thousands of kitchens opened by foreign relief organisations, where the children came for a meal every day, saved millions of little starving creatures from a cruel death. But clearly this is more a strategical measure for temporary procedure during the struggle than a method for permanent relief. Useful as it is where starvation is raging in all its horror, it tends to make the population into paupers when it is continued in districts where the scourge has become less dangerous.

It would be a very excellent thing if all the societies which are interested in the starving Russian children would go on helping them right up to the day when their country has been economically restored to such an extent that it can take over the whole responsibility. By aiding the Russian institutions for child-relief, providing the schools with means to distribute food among the children and helping the mothers to reduce the terrible child-mortality, they could give the proper completion to the relief work for the starving, which even though it was far from adequate, was nevertheless a fine gesture of international solidarity.

The great number of homeless children constitutes

one of the gravest problems in Russia to-day. The children are a nation's future ; their mental and bodily soundness will form the backbone of the coming generation ; but how is it with these homeless children, especially in the large Russian towns? The reports one receives on their condition are grim reading.

It may be conceded that the Soviet authorities have devoted much attention to this problem, and have done a good deal to mitigate the evil, but it has proved too much for the means which were available.

The Pan-Russian Executive Committee recently proclaimed a " Children's Week " at the beginning of May, with the object of collecting funds to save these multitudes of unfortunates. In that connection it was stated that many thousands of these poor little creatures are wandering about in the towns and in the country, in conditions of incredible suffering, want, and destitution. Thousands of them die by the roadside or in the streets from hunger and disease ; but what is still worse, crime and prostitution are increasing to a dangerous extent among these miserable little beings, and their lives are assuming the most unnatural and perverse forms. The state of things is so bad that it is now difficult to find among them a healthy child, or one who is really normal, physically and psychically.

The children's homes, in which more than a million orphan children receive shelter, have the greatest difficulty in procuring food and clothing for them; they cannot possibly house any more, and there are no funds to open new homes.

The Russian Soviet journals contain harrowing descriptions of the state of things among these waifs and orphans in the towns, whither they flock from the country. And from every town they beg and thieve their way to Moscow, where they have become a serious danger. It is estimated that 15,000 of them live in the deserted houses and cellars of that city. When they are taken to public children's homes near the city they run away again, and frequently entice a number of their new companions to escape with them.

The streets are full of hosts of little cigarette sellers, little beggars, little pickpockets and roughs, as well as little prostitutes. It is true, remarks one paper (the *Pravda* of Moscow) that we have no criminal statistics, but we know that fourteen and fifteen year old boys murder and plunder, and bring their booty to their mistresses, who are only twelve or thirteen years old. The keepers of some of the worst haunts of these criminal gangs have been found to be young boys of fifteen to seventeen. Agents of the Moscow Soviet, who have investigated the conditions, have found little girl prostitutes of ten or eleven years to whom the traffic in vodka (spirits) and cocaine was quite familiar.

Crime is increasing at an alarming rate among children. Nimble little hands snap up everything that is left unguarded even for a moment, and the "income" from this thieving is at once invested in spirits or cocaine, or gambled away. The illegal trade done by these children in spirits and narcotics (chiefly cocaine) is astoundingly large.

"This shows," says the *Isvestia,* "the decadence in our home life, in our education, in the growing unemployment, and in the general demoralisation of the people."

By request of the Moscow Soviet the Pan-Russian Executive Committee has taken steps to combat this evil, and has instructed the Extraordinary Commission (the Tcheka) to form a special children's tcheka, largely consisting of children below sixteen years of age, in order to deal with the child criminals.

Everyone knows that no plague is more catching than criminal epidemics such as this, terribly destructive as they are in their effects. And of course they are never so infectious and destructive as when they lay hold on the susceptible mind of the child. We have here a grave danger whose menace is not confined to Russia.

According to a report which I have just received from my representative in Ukraine, Captain Quisling, the conditions among homeless children seem to be very bad there, even though they may be less bad than those described above.

Out of Ukraine's 11 million children more than a million are orphans or semi-orphans. About 150,000 are in various children's homes or the like, where, however, the general state of things is unsatisfactory both as regards feeding and accommodation. The mortality is therefore very high, being up to 80 per cent. for new-born infants.

The number of children who have neither home nor anyone to look after them is probably about 100,000. They live a vagrant life, gathering chiefly in the neighbourhood of railways and about the stations, where they may be seen in flocks, ragged, frequently half naked, begging for a scrap of bread, and certain to become criminals if they do not soon die of starvation and hardship. In 1922, 12,204 criminals under fourteen years of age were registered.

The unsatisfactory conditions in the workmen's dwellings and the widespread unemployment affect the children in serious fashion. Hundreds of thousands of children are suffering in consequence ; but the state of things is particularly bad in the three southern famine districts : Odessa, Ekaterinoslav, and Donetz. Here there are altogether 3,900,000 children, of whom 1,800,000 are estimated to be more or less in a starving condition, while 600,000 are expected to die unless they can receive assistance.

To show what the position is like it may be mentioned that of the inmates of the children's homes in the Odessa province 35 per cent. are suffering from anæmia, 25 per cent. from debility, and 40 per cent. from tuberculosis.

The relief given to the poor children of Ukraine and Russia is very inadequate. And the means both of the Soviet organisations and of the foreign relief organisations are much reduced. The future still looks dark, therefore.

Although this book especially aims at drawing attention to the economic side of the Russian problem, I thought it right to point out thus briefly some directions in which I hope that work may still be done by all those who have been attracted to Russia by a feeling of simple humanity, because the land was devastated by a famine more cruel than history records. Their unselfish work has ameliorated great and awful suffering, and has helped to disperse the suspicion and hatred which still stand between Russia and the outside world.

CHAPTER XII

CONCLUSION

IN the foregoing chapters of this book I have endeavoured to portray the economic conditions of the country as objectively as possible. In order correctly to judge of the part which the Russian factor may play in restoring the equilibrium of Europe, one should avoid, on the one hand, underestimating its importance, while on the other hand one should equally avoid nourishing any illusions in regard to the present productivity and purchasing power of this vast land, occupying half of Europe and a large part of Asia.

I am convinced that the resumption of normal relations between Russia and other countries is imperatively necessary for the prosperity of both. But it would be most unfortunate were the new economic connections to be based upon a misconception of the real condition of Russia's trade, industry and agriculture, transport and finance.

I have pointed out the unfortunate measures and mistakes of the Soviet administration in a way which has perhaps surprised those who know the interest and sympathy with which I have followed the Russian Government's efforts to resuscitate this vast, unhappy country. On each occasion that the repatriation of war prisoners and the relief of the sufferers by famine have taken me to Russia, I have been received with a confidence and cordiality which have moved me greatly. This seemed to me to be one reason the more why I should say quite plainly what I thought of the situation, in the conviction that this frankness was alike in the interests of Russia and of Europe.

On my journeys in Russia and Siberia before the war I was struck by the riches of these enormous regions, by the important part they already played in the economy of Europe, and by their vast possibilities of development.

When I undertook the duties of High Commissioner for the repatriation of war prisoners, at the instance of the League of Nations, and assumed the direction of the European famine relief, in accordance with the proposal made at the Geneva Conference in August, 1921, I was not only influenced by the humanitarian aspect of this work, which would restore approximately half a million persons to their homes, and which would make it possible to save several million people from a cruel death.

I also felt very strongly that Russia's exclusion was causing a fatal disturbance of the equilibrium of Europe, and I gladly welcomed the opportunity furnished me through these tasks, of studying quite objectively, *sine ira et studio*, the conditions in this country, which the general public abroad only knows from contradictory and often mendacious reports. I must add, that I have not been able to come in contact with the Russian people without feeling strong sympathy for their endurance in suffering both before and after the revolution, and without admiring the primitive fortitude with which they have always taken fresh courage and renewed their efforts to improve their position.

The impression produced on me by my study of the different departments of economic life in Russia is that this great country has been suffering from a grave sickness, from which it is only just beginning to recover. Before 1914 the social life of Russia was not sound, and one cannot regard the regime of the Tsars as a normal form of Government. But the Great War quickly made the national malady worse. The revolutions in 1917, the foreign wars, and the civil wars between 1918 and 1921 marked the crisis, followed by convalescence, which, however, was greatly retarded by the famine which devastated the most fertile regions of the Volga and Southern Ukraine.

I am convinced that Europe and the whole world will gain by hastening and facilitating this convalescence. I believe that even without help from abroad the Russian Government is able, though very slowly, to improve the country's position, if the harvest is normal for the next few years. During several years Russia has vegetated, as it were; she will be obliged, so far as I can see, to reduce her industry still further, and will find great difficulty in coping with the deficit on it. By exercising great economy she will be able, I think, little by little to collect the necessary capital for restoring the country's prosperity.

But this process would be greatly accelerated, much to the benefit of Europe and Russia herself, if foreign industry and trade would co-operate in this work of reconstruction by giving on credit the machinery and products without which Russia's production cannot be increased.

The grave position of international finance obviously prevents foreign capital from giving Russia advances without security and *en bloc*. The money might even, perhaps, be used in ways which did not really increase the country's capacity for production, and the population's consequent ability to pay the money back and to buy. Moreover, the money might help to strengthen the nationalising and centralising tendency, and this would counteract the movement in the direction of free trading and economic independence which was initiated by N E P.

On the contrary, credit given to undertakings and special societies whose prospects and capacity for development had first been carefully investigated, would greatly improve the position of considerable sections of the population, and would open up possibilities which would interest foreign industries; while at the same time it would favour a general development, thereby helping to secure more normal working conditions for industrial, commercial, and agricultural enterprises. Strengthened by foreign capital, these enterprises would probably gain in independence and vitality, and this in turn would raise the general economic *niveau*. Certain railways, mining and industrial undertakings, and co-operative peasant societies would quickly begin to thrive, if they received credit in the form of goods.

I am not blind to the extent to which such a resumption of permanent economic relations is made difficult by the old Russian debt, which the Soviet Government has hitherto failed to acknowledge. I hope an understanding will be reached as soon as possible on this delicate question, which certainly forms the greatest difficulty in the way of Russia obtaining Government credit. But it seems to me that foreign industrial and business men might very well, and without incurring political difficulties, give credit in goods to the Russian societies and other enterprises. By restoring Russia's capacity to produce, one would give the country back its capacity to pay, and so render it easier to carry out a general and final settlement, which would have an important influence on every aspect of the vital problem of resuming normal relations. The chief difficulty to be overcome is the lack of confidence felt by foreign countries in regard to Russia, and the procrastination of the clumsy bureaucratic machinery by which the Soviet administration does its work.

The experience now being gained by my famine relief organisation will possibly help to restore foreign confidence in the feasibility and interest of participating in the work of Russian reconstruction.

In order to help the peasants in the famine districts, who are destitute of live stock and agricultural equipment, to recommence cultivating their land, we are establishing two model stations for agricultural reconstruction, one in Russia and one in Ukraine. Being furnished with a score of tractors (most of which are already on the way to Russia), repair outfits, and necessary implements, and in addition with a certain amount of working capital, each of these stations will be capable of farming a considerable extent of country. Under the direction of a foreign agricultural expert sent to Russia for the purpose, these stations will be run on an entirely commercial basis ; the peasants and co-operative peasant societies are to pay in corn, after the next harvest, for the work which is done for them. The income obtained will be entirely and exclusively devoted to relief in the famine districts. Detailed reports on the development of the stations, the difficulties encountered, and the results obtained, will be published at frequent intervals by our publicity office, thus enabling the industrial world outside to secure up-to-date information as to the conditions under which work may be done in Russia.

Our idea is that this reconstructive work, so necessary in order to help the population of the famine districts, shall continue until the summer of 1924, as far as our means permit, and in co-operation with the other philanthropic organisations. At the same time we shall give such aid as may be possible of a medical and sanitary kind, and to the universities and schools. Thus we shall endeavour, on a very modest scale, to participate in the economic restoration of the country.

What we really feel is that it is not enough temporarily to snatch the starving populations of the Volga valley and Southern Ukraine out of the jaws of death ; one must not desert them before providing them with the means to till their soil, and to manage by themselves. True humanity does not give merely temporary aid to stop the disease for a season, but seeks to help the patient right through, and does not give him up until he has regained his health and is able to resume his ordinary life. In order to carry out this programme of help for the population in the Russian famine districts considerable funds are necessary. We ourselves have not got them, unfortunately, but we are trying, by means of a concrete example, to show the way which we believe to be the right one.